ENTWISTLE

Clive R Walsh

Publication No 33   April 2011

No 33 Entwistle
Clive R Walsh
Published by Turton Local History Society April 2011
ISBN 978-1-904974-33-8

This book is dedicated to the memory of the late Ruth Anderson,
who made a very valued contribution to its contents.

TURTON LOCAL HISTORY SOCIETY

Turton Local History Society exists to promote an interest in history by discussion, research and record. It is particularly concerned with the history of the old Urban District of Turton, Lancashire and its constituent ancient townships of Bradshaw, Edgworth, Entwistle, Harwood, Longworth, Quarlton and Turton.

Previous publications of Turton Local History Society are listed on the inside front cover.

Meetings of the Society are held from September to May inclusive, beginning at 7.30pm on the third Tuesday of each month at the Barlow Institute, Edgworth. Visitors are welcome.

PREFACE

This book was researched and compiled over a period of several years by a working group of Turton Local History Society members including Clive Walsh, Sandra Isherwood, Kate Hopkins, Jill Bullough and the late Ruth Anderson. Many people assisted in this study but thanks are particularly due to Peter Harris for his work in compiling the book and to the following for providing valuable information

Mr & Mrs Alan Chamberlain, late of Edgefoot Farm
Mrs Pat Heron of Holly Bank, Entwistle
The late Mrs Eda Timms (nee Sharples) of Bixey Ford, Darwen
Mr & Mrs Alf Mitton, late of Entwistle Hall
Mr William Whitehead of Blackburn Road, Edgworth
Mr Mike Hatzar of Darwen
Mr & Mrs Cheadle of Armsgrove Farm, Turton

CONTENTS Page

CHAPTER 1   INTRODUCTION

Situated in the north eastern corner of Bolton-le-Moors Parish, Entwistle, a township of 1450 acres (statute) is bounded by the watershed between the Ribble and Mersey on the north side, by the old Bolton-Blackburn Turnpike (now A666) and part of Cadshaw Brook on the west, by Entwistle Reservoir and part of Bradshaw Brook to the south and on the east side by Broadhead Brook and Aushaw Moss. The central valley of Whittlestonehead Brook is overlooked by Black Hill on the west and Soot Hill to the east, both over 1000 feet high.

Although the Roman Road from Manchester to Ribchester passes through Entwistle, no artifacts from this period have been found in the township and the earliest definite records come from after the Norman Conquest.

The Manor of Entwistle, which has been spelled Hennetwistel, Ennetwysell or Entwysel, appears to have been formed during the early 1200s possibly from the Manor of Edgworth already held in part by the Entwistle family. The terms Old Livings and New Livings, used for various Entwistle farmsteads, are of ancient origin and may refer to farms established on the original estate as distinct from those of a later time.

From the earliest times, until the sales by the Tyldesley family, Lords of the Manor until after the Civil War, Entwistle was a remote and inconsequential part of Bolton Parish. At least a quarter of the township was occupied by two infertile upland wastes, Cranberry Moss and Aushaw Moss. The rest was mostly given over to small tenanted farms with a few cottages, together with Entwistle Hall where the Lord of the Manor traditionally lived.

During this period the inhabitants would have been largely self sufficient in food. They would have spun wool from local sheep, woven it on their own looms and perhaps produced some cloth in excess of their own need for sale. Any grain they produced would have been ground in the corn mill belonging to the manor. The nearest church would have been the chapel of ease at Chapeltown in the adjacent township of Turton, far more convenient than the distant parish church in Bolton.

However, the Civil War and Tyldesley's enthusiastic support for the losing side changed the nature of Entwistle by causing the old manor to be broken up and sold to some of the existing tenants. The families who bought their land holdings became a new force in the township. As yeomen freeholders they had a strong interest in maximising the returns from their activities and many of them became instrumental in the future developments.

The road system, until the end of the eighteenth century, consisted of the old Roman Road that passed through the eastern part of the township and the ancient Edge Lane that extended from Chapeltown through Overhouses, past Entwistle Hall and on over Cranberry Moss into Darwen. From near Entwistle Hall on Edge Lane was a connection to the Roman Road called Hob Lane. The Roman Road also boasted a short connection to the hamlet of Whittlestone Head and, from a junction near Wayoh Farm, Lee Lane ran over Broadhead and eventually to Haslingden. Otherwise there were only tracks joining farms that Yates thought unworthy of including on his map in 1786.

Initially the Industrial Revolution had little effect on Entwistle, except that the rivers of abundant clean water did attract the bleaching industry at an early date and eventually the water itself was collected into large reservoirs for use elsewhere. Because of Entwistle's location at a low point in the range of hills between Bolton and Blackburn, communications between these fast growing industrial towns were routed to pass through or close to it. The first of these was the turnpike that ran just outside the western boundary of the township. More important, in its impact on Entwistle, was the railway which apart from being an engineering feat in itself, stimulated some heavy industry in the township and in time brought a few affluent commuters who valued quiet country residences away from the smoke and bustle of the nearby towns.

This, in brief, is the story of Entwistle, the various stages of which are described in the following chapters, starting with the original manor and its lords and going on to cover the more important families who were able to acquire some freehold. The major settlements are then described as they are encountered along the main roads. Subsequently, each development resulting from the Industrial Revolution is examined in turn including Know Mill, the reservoirs, the railway and the major extractive industries (coal, stone and brick). Finally the provisions of the two Enclosures affecting Entwistle are briefly recorded and the concluding chapter details important families who settled or otherwise found themselves living in Entwistle during the last two centuries.

CHAPTER II   EARLY YEARS

2.1   THE ENTWISTLES, LORDS OF THE MANOR

The Entwistle family in England can be traced back to the 11th century when the
first members, recorded in 1067, were Sir John Entwistle (brother of the then
Lord of Hombie) and his two daughters.

The family then appear in the records as follows:-

> In 1276 *'Ellis de Entwisle'* was called upon to defend his title to twenty
> acres of woodland in Edgworth. Ellis said that his ancestors had held the
> pasture *'in severalty'* (sole tenancy of property) and his father had
> enclosed part of the common land.

> In 1283 and again in 1293 Ellis of Entwistle claimed that the Prior of the
> Hospitallers of St John of Jerusalem should acquit him of the service
> required by the Earl of Lancaster and of the fee tenement in Entwistle and
> Edgworth of which the Prior was Mesne Lord (one who held land of a
> superior, but had granted part of it to another person).

> Parts of Edgworth and Entwistle manors were in early times controlled
> by the Knights Templar until they fell into disfavour and their lands were
> confiscated in 1308 by Edward II (1307-1327). In 1305 the tythes of
> Edgworth were set by Richard Radcliffe at two marks (13s 14d) per year
> payable to the Templars. By 1312 after the Templars were dissolved,
> their property went to the King and some to the Knights Hospitaller.

> By 1312 *'Robert de Hennetwisel'* received two oxgangs or 60 acres of
> land in Edgworth as a dowry from his bride Elizabeth, a daughter of the
> great William Radcliffe of Radcliffe Tower, whose family, as Earls of
> Sussex, became the most powerful in the kingdom. Two oxgangs was a
> fourth part of the manor and quite possibly the township of Entwistle was
> established from this beginning as a detached part of Edgworth.

> In 1329 the Prior of the Hospitallers claimed from John Entwistle the
> service due for a messuage and 40 acres of land in Turton. This John,
> possibly a son of Ellis, also contributed to the subsidy of 1332.

> In 1351 William Radcliffe, son of the *'Great William'* held 12 oxgangs of
> land (360 Cheshire acres) in Edgworth, in thanage by service of 16s. 8d.
> payable to the Knights of St. John.

Following the demise of the Templars, Entwistle had become a Royal Manor in 1312. However for purposes of local administration the Salford Hundred had long been established and was divided into individual parishes, such as Manchester, Bury, Bolton, Middleton, Radcliffe and Rochdale. Entwistle was included in the Parish of Bolton le Moors which was one of the largest in the country. As the parish church was far away, local chapels were gradually established for the convenience of people in remote areas. The nearest of these to Entwistle was at Turton where a 'chapel of ease', was provided at Chapeltown by 1450. Before that, as church attendance was compulsory, the inhabitants would have had a long walk to attend church services every Sunday.

The Black Death, in the summer of 1349, resulted in widespread depopulation over the whole country, including large tracts of Lancashire. In the Salford Hundred it was estimated that one third of the population died. Robert de Entwissel's family, who had spent years in land clearance and making new enclosures, would have found it difficult to farm the manor with a much reduced workforce.

At this time Robert de Entwissel would still have been in a very privileged position. According to Norman law, he would be permitted to graze 4 oxen, 8 cows, 40 sheep and 2 horses on Edgworth Moor for each oxgang in his ownership and he enjoyed the use of meadows, wastelands and fisheries. On the other hand his landless serfs were expected to work for the Lord of the Manor at least four days a week, on jobs that included ploughing, sowing, harrowing, ditching, draining, harvesting and attending to cattle.

Many years later the record shows that Anyon Entwistle died in May 1442 holding a fourth part of the Manor of Edgworth by one sixteenth of a Knights Fee. This was c350 Cheshire acres and the service of 1s 3d a year, or a clear value of 20 shillings. He also held the Manor of Entwistle of St John of Jerusalem (Knights Hospitaller) by service of 12 pence a year. The clear value was 100 shillings including lands in Turton and Bolton. Anyon was the head of the family until his son Ellis Entwistle inherited the family estates when he was just twenty-three years old.

From the same family was Sir Bertine Entwistle, born at Entwistle Hall in 1395. The Victoria County History records that *'Sir Bertine Entwisell, Knight, Viscount and Baron of Bricqbel was a distinguished warrior in the reigns of Henry V and Henry VI. Bertine was amongst the heroes of Agincourt for which he received a knighthood and by his skill and valour contributed to the conquest of France. In 1450, when the Duke of Somerset lost Normandy, Bertine returned to Entwistle from France. Sir Bertine built Entwistle New Hall (Old Livings), sometimes called Bertine's Hall and later Lower House'.*

Sir John Antwysell's Coat of Arms.

Robert Hennetwyssel's Coat of Arms.

Sir Bertine Entwistle's Coat of Arms.

A cornet from Tyldesley's cavalry regiment with gold pelican and wreath on a red field.

Following the death of Henry V, Bertine became a faithful follower of King Henry VI and fought with him in the Battle of St Albans in 1455 under the banner of the Red Rose of Lancaster against the House of York. 800 Lancastrian men died including the Duke of Somerset, Sir Robert Vere, the Earl of Stafford and Sir Bertine Entwisell; many more esquires and fine gentlemen also perished. Bertine was buried in St. Peters Church, St Albans'.

2.2   KNIGHTS TEMPLAR AND HOSPITALLER

The Knights Templar, a military Order of knights, sergeants and chaplains was founded c1118 by Hugh de Peyens, a French knight, with headquarters in Jerusalem. Its primary objective was the protection of pilgrims en-route to the Holy Land. The Templars acquired their name from being granted their own temple by King Baldwin II, King of Jerusalem in 1099. Initially they were non-military, wearing a red cross on the left shoulder on a white full-length mantle without helmets or crests. They were well established in England in 1180 by which time the Order had been endowed with properties throughout western Christendom. During the crusades they rendered valuable service showing great bravery and devotion to duty.

The Old Temple in London was the 'Head House' in England from 1128 until replaced by the New Temple in 1184. By the early 1300s the Templars had some 50 houses throughout England. Two of them served as hospitals but most were centres for the management and farming of the Templars' estates and for recruiting new knights from the houses of the nobility. There were only 165 Templars in England in 1308, where their revenues amounted to £4,270 a year, and they rendered valuable service as bankers. The Master of the Templars was frequently summoned to Parliament and it was this role that ultimately caused their downfall as Kings and Popes grew jealous of their wealth and influence.

Frightful accusations were made against the knights and evidence of guilt was obtained by torture, leading to the dissolution of the Order by Pope Clement V in 1312. In England Edward II seized all the Templars' property some of which was conferred on the 'Hospitallers', although the best was disposed of for the benefit of Edward II and his Barons.

The Knights Hospitaller had been established in 1100 as the order of St John of Jerusalem. At first they were devoted to the aid of the sick, but afterwards became military monks in the Crusades. They adopted the Benedictine black habits with the eight pointed cross now worn by the modern 'St. John's Ambulance Brigade.' In 1309 they took the island of Rhodes but were expelled

Two Knights Templar sharing a horse, a symbol of the order's original poverty.

Knights Templar escorting pilgrims to Jerusalem: 19th century print.

James of Molay, last Grand Master of the Templars: 19th century engraving.

Burning of Templars: 14th century engraving

8

by the Ottomans in 1522. In 1530 the Emperor Charles V gave them the island of Malta which, as Knights of Malta, they held until 1798 when they were defeated by Napoleon. The Knights still survive to this day as a sovereign order with headquarters in Rome.

2.3   PROBLEMS OVER INHERITANCE

In 1544, long after the time of the Knights Hospitaller, another Entwistle called Edmund held, among other properties, the Manor of Entwistle from the King in socage by an annual rent of 12 pence. He also held land in Turton, Bolton, Radcliffe, Wayoh and Manchester.

In 1545 Edmund's eldest son called George, (aged 23 years) inherited a very substantial estate consisting of messuages and lands in Entwistle, Broadhead, Edgworth, Wayoh, Bolton, and Manchester. It was a large estate for one so young and after two law suits against his family and many disagreements, he began to sell parcels of his land and mortgage other substantial parts to a Mr George Garnett of London, a money lender.

In 1555 a large part of George Entwistle's estate was sold to Mr Thurston Tyldesley of Myerscough, near Lancaster and 'in there lies the root of the problem'. By 1571, with no mortgage deed and no bill of sale, there arose a dispute over ownership between George Garnett of London and Thurston Tyldesley which ended in the law courts. On the 30th September 1571 in the Duchy Court of Lancaster, with the Lord Chief Justice, Lord Derby, sitting in judgement, the verdict was given in favour of the Tyldesley family and Entwistle Hall became their legal property.

Many of the Entwistle family continued to live in the township as shown in the Protestation Return of 1642 (Appendix 1), which record *Alex Entwisley, Ellis Entwisley, Hugh Entwisley, John Entwisley junior, John the older, John the eldest, Ralphe, Thomas junior* and, *Thomas the older.*

Some of the Entwistle family became tenants of the Tyldesleys. The most prominent were Thomas Entwistle (son of Martin) deceased, tenant for three lives; John (younger son of Thomas deceased) and John (eldest son of John, the elder of Entwistle, yeoman). This John Entwistle, along with John Norbury (eldest son and heir apparent of Francis Norbury) purchased part of the Entwistle Manor from Edward Tyldesley Esq. in 1657, consisting of seventeen farms, houses, edifices, ways, water-courses, orchards, lands and meadows in Entwistle.

In the subsequent resale some weeks later only three Entwistle families bought properties out of the seventeen being sold. John Entwistle's son bought part of the Manor House, Hugh Entwistle bought Crow Trees and Thomas Entwistle bought an unnamed property. (This Thomas Entwistle became overseer of highways in 1667)

The Hearth Tax records of 1666 (Appendix 2) show that only four families named Entwistle (*Entwisley*) were wealthy enough to pay the tax. These were: *John Entwisley*, (who lived in part of Entwistle Hall), *3 hearths*; *Hugh Entwisley* (Crow Trees), 3 *hearths*; *Thomas Entwisley, 1 hearth*; *John Entwisley 1 hearth*. The record gives a good indication of the new families that had moved into the township since the Tyldesleys began to sell their properties. It seems that most of the old Entwistle families by this date had left the manor, although many became successful elsewhere, even famous, as lawyers, surgeons, churchmen, bankers, engineers or businessmen.

By 1795 in the Enclosure of Edgworth Moor, only three Entwistles are listed as freeholders and two as tenants in Entwistle manor. They are: James Entwistle, yeoman, Boltons Farm; John Entwistle, Old Livings, Old Ralphs Farm; John Entwistle, weaver, Entwistle; Thomas Entwistle, labourer, Bolton; and Betty Vickers (nee Entwistle), spinster of Tottington, who together owned Jacketmans Farm.

2.4   THE EARL OF DERBY AND THE TYLDESLEYS

The Tyldesleys who took over the manor from the Entwistles were under the patronage of the Earls of Derby. The Tyldesleys' lands came to them from the Earl who, soon after he received them from Henry VIII, allowed an estate at Myerscough to go into their possession.

'I King Lord Hendry VIII in 1526 by Deed off Grant.
1526 Feb 10th int To myn welbeloved S'vante, Edward Stanley, Erle of Derbei; I duss granted all the demayne lands, gardens, orchards, meadows, lesows, pastures, woods with all their appts, inc Mierscghe, Lancaster af'er parte of myn Royal Demacs, bye space off 3 life's to he'.

Four weeks later, from a letter from Earl of Derby:

Marchi 1526 A h're sent by myn Lord Stanley, Erle of derbei, & c.
To myn trusty e welbeloved S'vante Thurstani Tydesley, Squire.
I thuss of this daye granti hee al saede Landy's wthn the towny'sh off Mierscoghe yn Lancastshire: Unto the end & term of XXXyers e maore, then

next folowyng: He paying's the yerly rente accustom ffor the usual tymes: I will yt Jane, nowe my wif, shall have durying hir lif ye lodge in Myerscoghe to dwell yn durying hir pleasure;
Wryten at myn Manor of Lathom, this the XIX daye of Marchi 1526. 'I Edward Erle of Derbei':

This extract refers to Thurston Tyldesley acquiring land at Myerscough. Thurston Tyldesley of Wardley, (the eldest son of Thomas Tyldesley) married twice and from his will it would seem that he was much engaged in the affairs of the Derby family.

Thomas Tyldesley had been the Deputy Governor of the Isle of Man (Earl of Derby's property) and as such was responsible for collecting all taxes on the island together with the duties on imports and exports.

Thurston Tyldesley was a great hunter and fine horseman. Often he and his great friend Andrew Barton of Smithills Hall followed the chase over each other's land. Whittle, the historian, relates that lands in Entwistle abounded with game and that *'deer, hogs, wolves and foxes'* could be found there. Whittle also tells us that riding was the most common and comfortable way of travelling, for roads were few, in a very poor state of repair and in winter almost impassable.

2.5   EDWARD TYLDESLEY ESQ AND SIR THOMAS TYLDESLEY

From 1571 and through the next 85 years the Tyldesleys invested a considerable amount of time and money in developing new farms, tenements, smallholdings and the like in Entwistle. The Manor of Entwistle saw great changes. Thurston Tyldesley had his own legal attorney living permanently in Entwistle at Crow Trees, no doubt to oversee his new estate.

In 1617 King James I passed through Lancashire on his way from Scotland to London. He reached Hornby Castle on the 11th August and the following day was at the home of Edward Tyldesley in Myerscough. After hours enjoying the chase in the royal forest, he proceeded to Hoghton Tower (16th August) where he stayed for 2 days, then went on to be the guest of Lord Derby, at Lathom. This shows that the Tyldesleys were of high standing in the social scale, being closely associated with the Earls of Derby and known to the king..

John Parker, attorney at Law, acting for the Tyldesley family became High Sheriff of Lancashire in 1653. He lived at Lower House (Lower Crow Trees). A new wing was added sometime between 1555 and 1640, called *'Parker Living'*, to accommodate their attorney during the Tyldesleys' ownership.

During the Civil War Sir Thomas Tyldesley was one of the King's most loyal supporters in Lancashire. After taking Preston, Lord Derby advanced his army of about 5000 men up the Ribble in a concerted attempt to finally subdue the Parliamentarian Hundreds of Blackburn and Salford. Accompanying him was the cream of Lancashire's royalist officers, including Lord Molyneux, Sir Gilbert Hoghton and Sir Thomas Tyldesley of Myerscough.

In 1651 Lord Derby, with 1,500 men, gathered at Preston. Colonel Lilburne with the cavalry of Cromwell's New Model Army was encamped at Brindle to cover them. Many skirmishes occurred on August 22nd and 23rd and Colonel Lilburne then fell back to Hoghton Tower to await reinforcements. Lord Derby now thought the best chance of success lay with a rapid march south, taking Colonel Charles Worsley's infantry by surprise before they could join Lilburne's army at Hoghton Tower. The Parliamentarians realized what Lord Derby was up to and followed, catching them near Wigan on the 25th August. Despite the small numbers involved the battle was fiercely fought in cramped lanes and hedgerows. Though Lord Derby escaped, some of his best supporters were killed including Lord Widdrington, Sir William Throgmorton and the irrepressible Sir Thomas Tyldesley who was unhorsed, then shot dead.

Lord Derby, slightly wounded, fled south to join King Charles at Worcester, after hiding in the chimney of the Old Dog Inn, Wigan. Once again a fugitive, he finally surrendered to a Lancashire Captain called Oliver Edge of Bolton and was taken to Chester. There he was tried for treason and convicted. Despite several appeals he was executed at Bolton in the market square on October 16th 1651.

After the execution of Lord Derby, the most powerful Royalist in the north of England, the Tyldesley family fortune went into decline. Oliver Cromwell took a grip on the country and wealthy royalist followers, not surprisingly, kept a very low profile. Long before Cromwell's death in 1658, many royalists had been heavily fined or had their estates sequestered.

After Sir Thomas Tyldesley was killed, young Edward, his eldest son, ran the family estates but the Tyldesleys saw many lean times during the Commonwealth, hence the sale of part of their Entwistle property in 1657.

2.6   THE FIRST SALE

'Sale in 1657 between Edward Tyldesley on the one part to sell the first part too John Entwistle Snr & John Norbury of the second part. Part of the Entwistle Hall Manor For thee agreed summe off £911. 10/- lawful English monnys.'

This sale included farms then in the occupation of the following tenants: John Kay, yeoman; Hugh Entwistle; John Entwistle, son of Thomas decd; Frances Norbury; George Longworth; John Kay son of Alexander of Entwistle, husbandman; Richard Aspinall, son of John; James Aspden; Arthur Kay; Peter Kay; Ellis Greenhalgh, Whittlestone Head; John Brandwood, part of Entwistle Hall; Anne Greenhalgh, wife of Thurston Greenhalgh, decd; Andrew Knowles, brother of James; Thomas Entwistle, son of Martin decd; also John Kay, shoemaker, part of Entwistle Hall.

These tenants had previously agreed with John Entwistle Snr and John Norbury that they should 'bye in trust' for other residents on the estate. Within the space of one month all farms, tenements and allotments had been sold to the respective tenants, Frances Norbury being the first 'paying the sume of £240-0-0 good English Monnys fore thee purchase of thee messuages & tenements & herditaments hereafter grattede namelye called Overhouses Tenement'.

This was a milestone in the history of Entwistle. For the first time a large number of properties, came up for sale and were offered to the individuals who lived in them. Never again did one family have full control of the manor. Successful families such as the Brandwoods, Kays, Horrockses, Norburys and one or two Entwistles became the new owner-occupiers. At the time of the sale the occupations of the new owners were as follows: Roger Brandwood, stone mason; Roger Brandwood, the younger, corn miller; William Whitehead, coal miner; Amos Greenhalgh, thatcher; S Entwistle, blacksmith; William Horrocks, quarryman; James Kay, merchant [probably a wool dealer].

In 1658 'Sir Thomas Tyldesley's widow, Frances Tildesley of Myerscough and Briget eldest daughter of the said Frances transferred by rights of heirship all property in the Manor of Entwisle 'on the Fourthe day off Junie yn thee yeare of oure Lord God an'o d'mme to thee compu tac'en of thee equi'ox of Englande 1658' to Mr Edward Tyldesley, Esq of Morleys, eldest son of Sir Thomas Tyldesley, deceased.

Edward Tyldesley, (b 1635) had inherited all of the family estates in 1656, but even with the restoration of the Charles II in 1660, there was little change in Tyldesley fortunes. Promises made by King Charles to his loyal supporters in Lancashire were never honoured. It had been expected that Edward would receive a new type of Knighthood, the Order of the Royal Oak, but it never came. Also the Tyldesleys were expecting a gift of a large estate near Blackpool, which would have increased their family wealth considerably. When this didn't happen, more sales of properties in Entwistle belonging to the Tyldesleys were agreed and in all nine more farms and cottages were sold to the sitting tenants some weeks later.

2.7 THE SECOND SALE

Edward Tyldesley's second sale of his Entwistle property, together with two in Edgworth, took place in 1670. The sale document reads:

'This indenture, made the 23 July, in the 10th year of Charles 11 (1670), between Edward Tyldesley, Esquire of Morleys in the County of Lancaster of the one part, and Francis Norbury of Entwisle, in the said county, yeoman, and Richard Lowe of Holamby, within the same county, yeoman and moneylender, of the other part.
Witnesseth that Edward Tyldesley did by his indenture of sale made between Edward Tyldesley and Francis Norbury and Richard Lowe, in consideration of five shilling paid by Norbury and Lowe, sell to them all the hereditaments hereafter mentioned, with appurtenances, to have and hold, from the day before the date of the same for one whole year, yielding and paying therefore unto Edward the rent of one peppercorn upon the Ferst day of Saint Michael the ArchAngel, (if the same be demanded) that the sum of 5 shilling was paid;
Now this indenture further witnesseth that Edward Tyldesley Esquire, for the sum of £270 paid by said Norbury and Lowe, hath sold and confirmed unto said Norbury and Lowe, for ever, all that messuage and tenement and lands &c, belonging in Entwisle now in the tenure of Edward Fogg, Husbandman' [Fogg's Farm]; *'Also all that messuage &c, and lands in Entwisle now in the tenure of several occupac'ons of Alexander Kay husbandman and James Kay, son of Alexande'r.*(part of Entwistle Hall)

Altogether some seven farm properties in Entwisle and two in Edgworth were sold that day. These included the farms of John Wood, Henry Bolton, Ralph Longworth and Thurston Rostron. The Edgworth farm of Thomas Knowles, yeoman of Knowles Farm was also sold, which was at the bottom of Hob Lane and included the corn mill, later to become the Know Mill Bleaching Co.

The sale deed went on to include:

'all that cottage or little tenement with appurtenances in Entwisle in the tenture of John Bannister, husbandman, together with the rateable and proportionable parts of the wastes and commons in Entwisle and Edgworth, belonging to the Mannor of Entwisle. And all tythes of Corn and Grain &c. from time to time arising out of the said premises. Exceit, and always reserved out of this grant unto Edward Tyldesley, the Moiety, or one half of the coal mines lying within the commons of Entwisle, with liberty to search for, dig and get coals within the same commons, jointly with Norbury and Lowe. Also Edward Tyldesley doth grant unto said Norbury and Lowe to hold the chief Lord or Lords of the ffee or ffees by the rents and services of right accustomed'.

'In witness whereof the parties aforesaid sealed this day and year first above writton, Annogue Dom 1670.'

Edward Tyldesley, the principal of this transaction, was the eldest of ten children (3 sons, 7 daughters). He was married twice, first to Anne Fleetwood, daughter of Sir Thomas Fleetwood of Newton, Lancashire, and second to Elizabeth, daughter of Adam Beaumont Esquire of Whiteley. There were several children from the first marriage and one daughter from the second. His first son was called Thomas after his grandfather, Sir Thomas Tyldesley, and it was he who kept the family papers and records now included in 'The Tyldesley Diary'. Edward Tyldesley died in 1687 aged 52 years.

All the tenants mentioned in this deed of sale had tenancy agreements for three lives (99 years) signed in 1655 by Edward Tyldesley. The rents payable were: *'Ralph Ffogg, bastard son of Edward Ffogg, 10 shilling per year; James Kay rent (?); Thurston Rawstrone 8s. per year; Richard Greenhalgh, Ellis Greenhalgh and Elizabeth Greenhalgh, son and daughter, which so long live, rent 2s. 6d. per year; Henry Bolton, Alice his sister and Oliver Ffogg of Entwisle, husbandman, so long live, rent 5s. per year; Richard, Elizabeth and Anne Knowles, son and daughters of Thomas Knowles, the longest liver of them, 6 shilling per year; Thomas Longworth, 13s 4d. per year* [Longworth Farm]; *John Wood and Thomas Horwich of Turton, husbandman, the longer liver of them, yearly rent of 2 shilling."*

2.8 ENTWISTLE OLD HALL

Before leaving the Entwistles and Tyldesleys it is worth examining Entwistle Old Hall, the traditional residence of the Lords of the Manor, which dates from the time of the Entwistles but still bears many relics of the Tyldesleys. The building is of stone construction, has a split flag roof and a central entrance hall with east and west wings. The entrance hall ceiling boasts an impressive plaster genealogical plaque in bold relief depicting a central spray of flowers surrounded by oak leaves, four 'Roses of Lancashire' plus acorns and daisies. It has been said to date from early Norman times, but quite possibly is a relic of Tyldesley ownership, as it includes a motif of a bird, possibly a pelican; which Tyldesleys had on their Coat of Arms.

In the hallway was a plank bench or seat, said to be used by tenants when the annual court leet was held by the Lord of the Manor. In a room to the right is an inglenook, with a heavy oak beam over the fireplace, originally used as the kitchen. The lofty room on the left of the entrance hall is the dining hall with a massive oak beamed ceiling. For many years it contained a huge, very finely carved black oak dining table. Behind is the Court Leet room, which would have been furnished with oak benches. There are various moulded oak beams throughout the Hall; all without carvings.

There were originally twelve spacious rooms on the ground floor but the Tyldesleys converted the Hall into a loom factory to provide work for the poor and needy. Roger Brandwood, Constable of Entwistle at that time, would have been responsible for their welfare and for dispensing the poor rate (1621).

The south facing front of the Hall still has many Tudor features including three and four light, mullion windows complete with dripstone headings. The main entrance door is surrounded by a massive stone overmantle. The north gable is topped by a large kitchen chimney stack. Tudor ball finials on each corner enhance the Hall's original appearance.

Entwistle Hall c1920.

Sir Bertine's
sideboard.

Sir Bertine's bedstead.
Together with the above
sideboard, these items were
originally part of the furniture
at Entwistle Hall and are now
at Turton Tower.

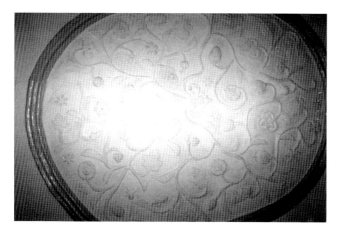

Plaster ceiling
from the entrance
to Entwistle Hall.

Sir Thomas Tyldesley.

Lower Crow Trees.

CHAPTER III   BRANDWOODS THE MASTER BUILDERS

3.1   OLIVER BRANDWOOD JUNIOR

The Brandwoods were quite possibly the most successful family in Entwistle to benefit from the sale of the Tyldesley estate. Early records list them as tenant farmers in the 1500s and their signatures appear on numerous wills and leases as befits a family of standing in the community. In 1560 Oliver Brandwood Jnr was the first to rent part of Entwistle Hall from old Edward Tyldesley after the Tyldesleys had obtained one half of the Manor of Entwistle in 1555.

In Oliver's will of 9th July 1607 a curious memorandum was inserted after all his money had been divided between his children in amounts ranging from 3 sh 4d to £30. *'I Oliver appoint my eldeste sonne Rodger Brandwood my sole executor as my easpeciall trust ye in hym, I the saide testator did take mye tenement ofe old Mr Edward Tyldesly for mye owne life also my wyffes life and for life ofe Rodger Brandwood mye sonne and yee longest liver ofe vs in the P'nes* [presence] *ofe said old Oliver Brandwood of Edgworth* [his father] *and others. When my sonne Rodger was married we whent to old Mr Edward Tyldesly a'd told him off the said marriage a'd he had us goe to his sonne Thomas Tyldesly a'd so wee dide a'nd gave too him XIIs* [shillings] *to bring in the wyffe off my sonne Rodger Brandwood.'*

It was common in Tudor times to rent a property for a term of 3 lives or 4 lives, each life being the equivalent of a 30 or 40 year tenancy. Oliver made sure that his lease extended to include the life of his daughter-in-law Mary Brandwood.

3.2   ROGER BRANDWOOD, CONSTABLE OF ENTWISTLE

The same Roger Brandwood, son of Oliver, became Constable of Entwistle in 1599 and was expected to oversee the poor under the Act of 1597. A constable was appointed annually in each township and the law required him and the overseers to levy a rate on every householder to provide food and shelter for the old, sick and infirm of the township.

The Great Poor Law of 1603 prepared by Sir Thomas Egerton provides that overseers and constables of townships were to meet monthly to provide employment for those paupers fit and able to work, by building walls, repairing roads and building cottages on waste land. Anyone refusing to work was to be denied Poor Law relief.

Constables also had the power to board out infants who had no family to support them, to apprentice poor children over the age of 7 years, to bring punishment to the idle poor and to return beggars, rogues and vagabonds to their parishes of origin.

From 1603 to 1609 large towns and some cities began to construct *'Houses of Correction'* or workhouses where constables had the power to place poor people with expenses paid out of the Poor Rate. Many of these workhouses would have a workshop attached to them. In 1603 the crown ordered the landowners of Lancashire to pay their 'Poor Rate Tax' at once or appear before the Privy Council at Lancaster.

There were two years of poor harvests in Entwistle between 1621 and 1622. As a result food became very expensive, great hardship was felt by the poor of the township and there were cases recorded of people actually starving. For relief even the Hall was turned into a loom factory to provide much needed work.

3.3   THE BRANDWOODS 1642-1826

In the Protestation returns for Entwistle of 1642 (Appendix 1) only two Brandwoods are listed: Oliver, grandson of Oliver Junior of Entwistle Hall, and his son Roger. In the Hearth Tax records of 1663 for Entwistle (Appendix 2), two Brandwoods are listed: Roger Brandwood, of Wayoh Hall, Lower Crow Trees, with four hearths and John Brandwood (his brother) of Entwistle Hall with one hearth (by this time the Hall had been divided into three parts).

By 1657 the Brandwoods had established themselves as prominent local business people in Entwistle. John Brandwood, grandson of Oliver, was wealthy enough to purchase the central part of Entwistle Old Hall from the Tyldesleys in 1657 and the family became the new Lords of the Manor of Entwistle. The first Lord was Roger Brandwood, (1657-1678) and subsequently Roger, his son, (1678-1707), then James Brandwood, eldest son of James (d 1715) followed by Roger, the second son, until 1761. Then Roger's only child, Ann Brandwood, married Christopher Baron and he became Lord of the Manor.

The Brandwoods established a thriving local building enterprise. They contracted to build farmhouses, barns, cottages, loom workshops, roads and bridges in Entwistle, Edgworth, Quarlton, Egerton, Chapeltown, Turton and as far afield as Blackburn, and Westhoughton. In 1690 one of the Brandwoods was living in 'The Dower House', or 'New House', now 'Entwistle New Hall' (2011).

Two Brandwoods were assessed for the Poll Tax in 1678 (Appendix 3). Roger, his wife and children paid 5 shillings and John, his wife and one child paid 3 shillings. In later Poll Tax returns only John is present because Roger Brandwood had died. Among the bequests in his will, dated January 1678, were:

'Yee testator gives his Messuages and Co in Wayoh in Entwisle [Lower Crow Trees] *containing Fowerscore acres off land to mye eldest sonne James Brandwood provided that the stone staynes in my dwelling at Wayoh are not defaced or removed, which I have often charged mye sonnes not to suffer to be done, But if this breach were madde, the testator demanded that the delinquent shoud fforfeit Ten pounds, to be divided amongst thee other children of thee donor. Mye will to be divided in three equell parts, one part mye wyffe Mary, Seconed part bequeath to Lawrence, William and Christopher my sonnes & Alice mye daughter equally divided amongst them.'*

The third part commonly called the death part reads:

'I give & bequeath as follows, to James mye eldest sonne two'e Cubboads, onne Presse [chest], *thee long table of the house and fourme belonging it, a stoole there, the Chimny P* [spits, brasses, fenders, kettles etc] *now in thee house with tongues spit & rack belong to it...One great Arke that be in the kitchen laffe* [round top large chest]. *To Rodger mye sonne one plain Bedsted and bed cloathes belongin itt (Exepting ffeather bed). To every onne off mye children I give ffive shillings apeac I remitt to John Bendwood* [sic] *mye sonne tenn pounds offe debte he oweth me by bonde; I give Alice mye daughter tenn pounds. I give towards the augmentery of the Chappell stock at Turton off the Ministry there off Thirty Shillings. All goods I give & bequeast to Lawrence & Christopher Brendwood mye sonns & Alice Brandwood mye daughter equaily amongst them divided: I nominate & appoint James Brandwood mye sonne sole executer of this mye Will hoping hee Faithfully execute same as mye Trust in hym reposed.*
Sealed signed in the precence of - William Horroskes, Christopher Horrockes (his mark), Tom Ainsworth (Aterny) Maie 30th 1679.

The total value of Roger Brandwood's Estate was £834 14s 6d.

The full inventory of this will is missing, but J.C.Scholes in 1882 calls it a singular production, being written on a slip of parchment about 1 yard long and 6 inches wide.

On the 10th of May 1707 Roger Brandwood, greatgrandson of Oliver Brandwood Junior died. His family were no longer rent paying tenants but property owning farmers and businessmen in their own right. His will reads:

21

'I Rodger Brandwood off Entsil Parrish of Boulton Le Moores, Yeoman. I stand sized in mey Demisne as of ffee in one Massuage & Tenement liying in Entisil commonly called bye the name of Entisl Hall, which I give to bequeath unto James Brandwood mye eldest sonne and hee shall paye thee som of one hundred and twenty ppounds of good and lawffull moneys of England fore my children too dwel together fore thee space off two yrs next insueing and Rodger Brandwood My second sonne shall carefully looke aft'r the rest of my young children for the space off tow years that mye eldest sonne James Brandwood take care of mye three youngest children till the youngest off them shall attaine the age off seventeen years. And as concerning mye personall estate I give unto Rodger Brandwood my second sonne, the sume of twenty ffive pounds; unto John Brandwood my third sonne, the sume of twenty ffive pounds; I give unto Mary Brandwood mye Daughter the sume of twenty ffive pounds; It is mye will that three ffive pounds which is above twenty pounds apeese bee deducted out of mye p'sonall estate and that the rest of mye personall estate togath'r with one halph of the one hundred and twenty pounds be equally to divided amongst mye three youngest children, Crsitwell, William, and Margret.'

'I nominate and appointe James Brandwood and Rodger Brandwood mye sonnes Executors of this mye Last Will and Testament.'

'Sealed Signed and Delivered In the sight and Presence of us- Rodger Brandwood [son], *John Brandwood* [brother], *James Bradwood* [brother],. *Ellin Knowles (Aterny)'.*

All the executors were illiterate and 'made their mark', only the attorney signed. Roger Brandwood died five days later on May 10th 1707, 62 years old and his heirs would have had to pay the equivalent of inheritance tax. John and James were his brothers and John died in April 1740 aged 86.

The ages of Roger Brandwood's children in this will were: Mary 31, James 26, Roger 23, John 20, Cristwell 16, William 13 and Margret 10. James Brandwood would have to look after the three younger children for 7 years until 1714 when Margret reached the age of 17.

The inventory attached to Roger's will reads as follows:

'A true and perfect Inventory of goods and Chattels and Personall Estate of Rodger Brandwood late of Entwistle Hall in the County of Lancaster yeoman decd apprised by us James Brandwood sen'r, John Postlethwhite, John Brandwood, and Andrew Knowles, twenty fourth day Maie 1707 as followeth:

	£	s	d
Item in *Bease* [cattle]	*13*	*0*	*0*
one horse	*3*	*0*	*0*
in *Bedding*	*3*	*0*	*0*
one *Arre-* [domed lid chest]		*10*	*0*
Three Chisses-[small chests]		*10*	*0*
in *Pewter and brass*		*10*	*0*
one *Table and Cupboard*		*10*	*0*
Pair Chairs		*4*	*0*
Capogears for a horse –[harness]		*5*	*0*
His Apparell	*3*	*3*	*0*
in *Hussellment-*[minor household goods]		*5*	*0*
The sum total	*24*	*17*	*0*

James Brandwood Sen'r, John Postlewhite (Attorney at Law), *John Bendwood his mark* (brother), *Andrew Knowles his mark.*

John Brandwood Sen died in 1784. In his will, dated 17th March 1784, he left Higher House Fold to his son John Brandwood Jnr, subject to a payment of £100 *'to mye daughter Marye. To mye sonnes William and Thomas I leave New House, also part of the land belonging to that part of the Old Hall late owned by Christopher Baron, this plot known as Sanderfield'.* John Brandwood junior was overseer of the poor in 1797 and died in 1799. The youngest son James was disinherited because he had joined the Society of Friends!

James Brandwood (1739-1826) was born at New Hall. He became known as the Steward of Turton and was one of the Commissioners appointed for the enclosing of Edgworth Moor in 1795 and Harwood Common in 1797. He joined the Society of Friends in 1761 and a formal account in the Rossendale Preparative Meeting Book where Minute 4 for the 15th of the 11th month reads:

'This day Joseph Kershaw, Samuel Haslam, Thomas Thomasson, John Wood and James Brandwood all of Entwistle in the Parish of Bolton who have for some considerable time frequented our Religious Meetings and also our meetings for Discipline and being Convinced of Friends principles they are desirous to join in Society with us; They therefore laid before this meeting a written paper signed by each of them signifying the same; which paper was first read, approved and ordered to be Presented to our next monthly meeting by our Representatives according as it was by them directed.'

James Brandwood soon took an active part in the affairs of the Society of Friends and for over 50 years was a 'minister' of that body. He preached in various parts of the country travelling to the new Rossendale meeting house, to the chapels in Edgworth, Crawshawbooth, Preston and as far afield as Huddersfield to practice his new religion. For this he became an outcast to his family and was excommunicated from St Peter's Parish Church, Bolton. He was the first to farm Pleasant View Farm Entwistle, called 'Brandwoods Farm' on the census of 1801.

James's working life was spent as a builder. He was plainly a man of outstanding talent and during his working life kept most detailed account books, containing plans of new buildings, repairs to old ones, road repairs and other sundry matters. A typical example from James Brandwood's account book reads: '*September 1805 paid to Mr Yates (Millwright) the sum of £1 3s 4½d, for Water Wheel buckets and repairs*'.

At the time of his death in March 1826 he had made his home in Westhoughton and was interred in the burial ground attached to the Quaker meeting house there.

Armsgrove Farmhouse, built by the Brandwoods c1700. Although now in Turton, Armsgrove was originally part of Entwistle Manor.

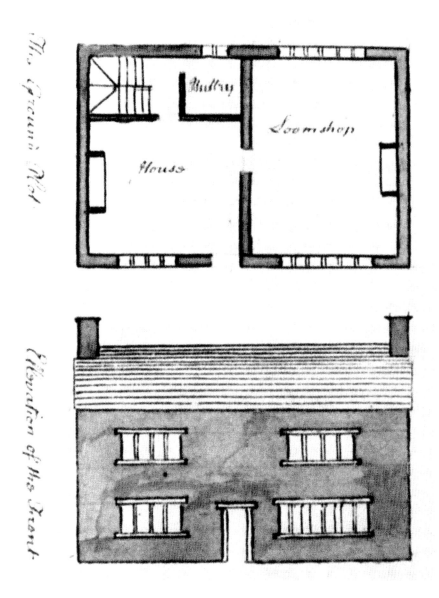

Original plan of Armsgrove House: note the downstairs
loomshop with large windows at the front and back.

No. 86 - Expence of rebuilding the Armygreaves Barn
which fell down 5 may? 1811.

	£	s.	d.
To expence of taking down the old Walls, and digging the new Groundworks 12 days work	1	11	0
To getting Wallstones to join with the old ones	2	16	8
To Cash pd Hird Entwisle for Carting Wallstones	4	5	0
To Do pd Thos Mullin and others for carting Sand	0	18	0
To 38 Windles of Lime laid down at 2/6 pr	4	15	0
To 36 Days mason work by Enoch Low at 3/6	6	7	9
To 34½ Do Do by Wm Low 3/6	5	19	0
To 40 days Labourers and Mason's work by Jas Brandwood Jun at 2/6 pr	5	0	0
To 60 days mason's and Labourer's work by Robt Mayoh at 3/0	9	0	0
To 35 days Labourers work by Jno Mathor 3/0	5	5	0
To 34½ Do Labourers work Isaac Entwisle 3/0	5	3	6
To 30½ Do Do Do Jno Howorth 3/0	4	11	6
To 36 Do mason's work by Wm Brandow 3/0	5	3	0
To Carpenters work	12	10	0
To Cash paid Thos Thomason for Slate, Loftings Flags and Baskin stones and Carting them	7	17	10
To Two Hundreds of Slating Lath's 7/6	0	15	0
To Slating 11 days at 3/0 pr	1	13	0
To 5 qr of Ridging stones at 1/8 pr	0	8	4
To Lath nails, Thumps and other Nails	0	12	6
To Door Hangings and other Iron work	1	14	2
To expence of carting Timber from the sawpit	0	12	0
To expence of Lime hair and work in pointing the Roof	3	6	0
To expence of clearing away Rubbish and other finishing work	2	14	8
To Cash paid for Ale given to workers at several times	0	8	6
To Do paid for Meal and Liquor at the laying and rearing	1	5	10
	£95	3	3

James Brandwood's account for rebuilding Armsgrove Barn in 1811.

	£	s.	d.
To Cash pd Joseph Low for Chimney pieces, Steps and Windowstones		17	6
To do. pd Wm Low for 45 yards of Flags 2 6	5	12	6
To do. pd Ralph Isherwood and others for Slate	10	6	6
To do. pd Margt Entwistle for carting flags and other Stones from Edgworth Delf	1	16	6
To do. pd Jas Kay for 62 Windles of Lime laid down 2/6	7	15	
To do. pd Jas Leach for 12 cartloads of Sand 1/0		12	
To do. pd Jas Kay for carting said Sand	1	4	
To do. pd at Bolton for a Sand Riddle		2	4
To do. pd Thos Livsey for Door check Pikes		1	5
To do. pd for Ridging Stones 9½ yards and carriage		17	6
To do. pd for Meat and Drink at the Rearing	1	1	7
To do. pd Jas Ormerod for some Window Stones		6	4
To do. pd for Lath nails and Stumps		7	6
To do. pd Fielding and Joshua for getting more stones	2	18	
To do. Jno Howard on account towards mason's work	14	10	3
To do. pd Jno Harris and others for filling up the stone pit	1	8	6
To do. pd Wm Low for 10 yards more flags at 1/6		15	
To do. pd Thos Thomasson for some Border Stones		4	
To do. pd Thos Brindle for getting some walstones flags etc		10	
To do. pd Ralph Isherwood for Slating	2	13	6
To do. pd for 4 Cart loads more Sand and Carting		12	
To do. pd for Sharpening at Walmsley Smithy		1	3
To do. pd W Knowles for flaging 43½ days at 3/0	2		6
To do. pd for Carting Slate from Edgworth	1	8	
To do. pd for getting Stones for Coalhouse etc	3	9	10
To do. pd Jas Kay for 24 Windles of Lime for Plaister	3		
To Cash paid Thos Crompton for an Ash Grate		4	
To do. pd Jno Howard on account towards Mason's work	7	3	
To do. pd to Thos Allen and others for forming the Garden Ground		10	8
To do. pd Joshua Clough for do. and walling	1	15	
To do. pd Thos Thomasson for Door Checks, flags and other Stones for the necessary and Garden wall	2	16	4
To do. pd Jno Smith for 11½ yards of Ridging stones at 1/6 £0 17 3 — and carriage £0 3 0	1	0	3
To do. pd Wm Knowles for dressing and setting Scuflings and Coopings on the Garden wall 4 days at 3 0		12	
To do. pd at Walmsley Smithy for sharpening for flagors			6
To do. pd Jno Horrocks for Ale for Workmen	5	14	2
To do. pd Saml Marsh for Malt and Hops		18	1
To do. pd the Carpenters for their other work	10	6	
To do. pd Wm Crankshaw for Nails for Flooring etc		13	4
To do. pd Thos Crompton for Hinges Handels etc		16	3
To do. pd Thos Brindle for some Stones for Garden wall		5	6
To do. pd Wm Bamber for Boards Tearing joists etc —			
To do. pd do. for Tearing Laths	3	10	
To do. pd for Tearing Nails	1	2	6
To do. pd Luke Booth for Plaister work	8	0	9
To do. pd for Paint and Painting	1	4	6
To do. pd W. Gordon for Glass windows	7	6	0
To do. pd Jas Hamer for 38 Strikes of Hair	1	11	8
To do. pd Wm Crompton for Grates Oven and Boiler	6	0	10
To do. pd Jas Kay for 23 Windles of Lime	2	17	6

Transcript of one of James Brandwood's detailed accounts.

Entwistle New Hall in 2006, originally built in 1697.

Higher House Fold Barn, part of the Tyldesley Estate, built 1555-1657.

Pleasant View Farm: built in 1801 on Cranberry Moss and originally called Brandwood Farm.

Brandwood's splendid barn at Entwistle Old Hall.

CHAPTER IV   THE KAYS OF ENTWISTLE

4.1   THE KAYS

One family that has certainly had a great deal of influence in the Manor of Entwistle is the Kays. In the Protestation return for Entwisle in 1642 there are eight men of that name (Appendix 1). In contrast to the return for Edgworth where only one of the 46 names is a Kay, which shows that Kays were predominantly an Entwistle family. The first to be recorded is a Mr John Kay in 1635 who rented part of Entwistle Old Hall from the Tyldesleys as a new tenant for 'three lives'.

In November 1655 James Kay, yeoman, was living in part of Entwistle Old Hall as a tenant of *'Old Edward Tyldesley'* of Myerscough. When the Tyldesleys sold part of the Manor in 1657 no less than 5 of the 17 tenements were acquired by members of the Kay family. These were John Kay (yeoman), Peter Kay, John Kay (son of Alexander of Entwistle), Arthur Kay and John Kay, (shoemaker and constable in 1661).

May 1661 was another milestone for the family: *'This agreement made between James Aspden of Entwisle etc and John Kay* [son of Alexander Kay] *of Entwisle* being a *conveyance of Four closes lying on the North East side of the said 'Aspdens House', being Whitacar's tenement Edg Rd,* [Edge Lane], *called the Green Field, the Rushey Field, the Green Field Hill* [Bertine's Hill] *and the Whiddlestone. As follows – sealed signed and delivered with this agreement that the within named John Kay, his heirs &C, forthwith in granted premises and all taxes and all lays after the rate and proportion of 'three farthings', quinden or fifteen and no more. And that James Aspden, his heirs &C, will hereafter free and discharge the said John Kay, his heirs &C from the office of Constableship of Entwisle for within-granted premises and from all charges and from all incumbrances relating to the same office.'* [John Kay was buying his way out of the public office of Constable.] *'These presents were sealed and delivered in the presence of John Entwisle, Hugh Entwisle, Henry Knowles, John Key, Thurston Smethurst and Jer Ainsworth, Atterny, Maie 1661.'*

The Kays, with thrift and industry, worked, bought and sold many farms in Entwistle Township in the following years, including: part of Entwistle Hall, Higher Crow Trees, Lower Crow Trees (Lower House), Whitacres, The Edge, New Hall, Overhouse Tenement, Higher House Fold Farm, Wayoh Fold Farm and Edgefoot Farm. As time went on they were clearly tending to buy the more expensive properties.

The 1666 Hearth Tax return for Entwistle records John Kay with 2 hearths, Alexander Kay, John Kay and Peter Kay with one hearth each. By 1673 Alexander and the elder John Kay had been replaced by Martin Kay and James Kay (Appendix 2).

On the 10th September 1670, Thomas Kay, husbandman, bought his birthplace, The Edge, Entwistle, a small tenement for which he paid the Tyldesleys the sum of £43. In late 1670 James Kay, farmer, son of Alexander Kay, husbandman bought more property from the Tyldesley estate. They were obviously becoming a family of some substance.

Peter Kay, as a freeholder in Entwistle, was able to increase his land holdings in 1672 by enclosing common land on Edgworth Moor. In his will of 15th Jan 1678 his effects were valued by Henry Berry, Francis Norbury (son of Francis), Ralph Entwistle, John Kay and Thomas Thomasson.

In 1678, the Poll Tax return for Entwistle included: James Key, 1 shilling; Widdow Key and her daughter, 2 shillings; Peter Key and his wife and one son, 3 shillings' (Appendix 3).

4.2   JAMES KAY OF TURTON

Born in 1774 at Edge Fold Farm, James Kay rose from humble beginnings to eventually become Lord of the Manor of Turton. He bought the estate from the late Sir Humphrey Chetham in 1835 and then took up residence in Turton Tower. He became a man of great wealth owning cotton mills in Preston, Bolton and Pendleton and bought many farms and cottages in his native Entwistle.

It is recorded that he would spend many a day walking in Entwistle calling at cottages and farms to reminisce with his old school friends over past times. It was traditional for all his tenants to pay their rents once a year at Turton Tower where James Kay would treat them to a splendid lunch with copious amounts of ale. On one such day his steward remarked that one tenant always came for the meal but had not paid his rent for 3 years, pleading 'old age and poverty'. After the meal James Kay approached his old school friend and asked him about the rent. Back came the reply that his cottage was so old and decrepit that it was not worth paying rent for and if he (Mr Kay) was not careful he would go and live elsewhere, much to the amusement of all present. Needless to say the old gentleman continued to live in his cottage until he died.

CHAPTER V   OTHER ENTWISTLE FAMILIES

5.1   THE NORBURYS

In the seventeenth century the Norburys seem to have been the outstanding family in Entwistle. Coming from a prominent old Cheshire farming family one of them married an Entwistle. They soon rose to prominence becoming constables and overseers of the poor on several occasions.

John Norbury, the younger, was entrusted with the purchase of part of the Tyldesley estate in 1657 which he then sold on to the sitting tenants. A few years later in the Hearth Tax returns of 1666 Francis Norbury is credited with 7 hearths, by far the largest number owned by anyone in Entwistle at that time.

Their main residence was at Overhouses where the family lived for five generations until the male line died out. Most of the property was then bought by members of the Brandwood family who continued to expand the Overhouses estate.

5.2   THE WHITEHEADS

From the late 1600s the Whitehead name is recorded on various leases and as a witness to wills. They seem to have established the family by marrying into the Brandwood and Entwistle families and one David Whitehead became township constable three times in the 1670s. He is also listed in the Hearth Tax returns and was assessed for the Poll Tax at 3 shillings. The preferred employment in the family seemed to be centred around coal mining and the livestock trade. Most of them seemed to reside in Edgworth.

5 3   THE BRIGGS

The Briggs family can trace their history in Entwistle only as far back as 1757 to a Miss Jane Briggs (Innkeeper of Edgworth), but they nevertheless soon became widespread:

'Witness of Sale, Sept 1st 1757 as a condition off a Bargine made between Mr Will'm Kaye off Entwisille (Slater) & Miss Jane Briggs innkeeper, (singl woman), Witnesseth that thee summe of xxx poundes English moneys two bee paid two Will'm Kaye on 1st Maie next & St Micals Daye followinge, bye Jane Briggs. Will'm duth agree two transffr & releae al hys rights, title & interests

of onne cottage & other buildinges with onne garten pluss a small parcel of lande belonging sitiuate at Thee Edge yn Entwisille,' [Edge Farm].

Later Jane married Joseph Kay, carpenter of Entwistle and lived at Edge Farm. They had two sons, Joseph Jnr and Arthur. Jane died and was interred at St Anne's, Chapeltown on the 23rd May 1770, the very same day that her infant child Arthur was baptized. Sadly he also died and was buried a week later.

Her remaining son, Joseph, went on to receive an excellent education at a private school in 'Olden Fold'. Later as a young man he went into an engineering business with his step-brother James Kay. Theirs was said to be the first machine workshop to be established in Bolton and was situated at the top of Silverwell Street. It was later recorded by Jane Briggs, Joseph Kay's surviving niece, that Kay's firm was *'the first to join a Samuel Crompton's spinning mule to the engine combined, in Bolton or elsewhere.'* The machine was placed in Mr Carlyle's Cotton Mill, situated off Bradshawgate, Bolton.

Another Briggs, Robert, a farmer, was born at *'Jack'O'Mans'* (Jacketmans) Whittlestone Head in 1765. He was the eldest son of George Briggs, another farmer, and Sarah. Robert's son John (1796-1871) married Molly Howarth of Edgworth and with her had 10 children. In 1820 he was a farmer and jobbing builder at Lower House Farm and for four years from 1832 worked on the new Entwistle Reservoir as an 'overlooker'.

John's son George Briggs (1823-1890), was also employed at the reservoir as a puddler in 1832 earning 2 shillings a day, and became an earth mover at 3 shillings a day in 1836. He married Alice Howarth in 1851 and after she died Jane Hilton in 1867. George and Jane lived at Lower House Farm, Entwistle, complete with several children, including those from his first marriage. By 1881 George had become a widower again and was living with eight of his children at New House Farm, Edge Lane where he died in 1890 after a lifetime of farming, two wives and eleven children.

John's youngest son William, a farmer, and his wife Nancy, a weaver, were living at Lower House Farm in 1881 with their surviving children. Their fifth child, Martha Ann (1880-1954), married Mr William Harold Lees (of Turton) on 2nd June 1906 at St Anne's Church.

Dorothy Briggs (b 1860) was the fifth child of George Briggs. She married John Yates (millwright) of Edge Farm, at St Anne's, Chapeltown and went to live at Know Farm at the bottom of Hob Lane. Later they moved to Edgefold Farm, Edge Lane with their four children, of which only John (b 1890) continued to farm after service in World War I.

33

Other Yates included George Yates, born in 1811 at Whittlestone Head. In 1880 he lived with his wife Elizabeth (74 yrs) and his grandson George (16 yrs) at Wallbank Farm. His son George (39 yrs), wife Ann and five children remained at Whittlestone Head in Old Lane Cottage.

George Briggs (junior), son of George (senior), married Alice Duxbury of Entwistle and lived at Entwistle Hall Farm with their four children.

Martha Ann Briggs' younger brother William (junior) (1889-1955) was born at Edge Fold farm and orphaned at the age of 6 yrs. At 12 yrs old he was working 5 hrs a day at Know Mill; during which time he was living with another sister Mary Briggs, school teacher, at Lower Hob Lane Cottages until he joined the army in 1914. When the war ended in 1918 he returned to Entwistle, to work at Know Mill as a machine tenter in the cloth drying department mainly on the night shift. He married his childhood sweetheart, Alice Whipp, at St Anne's Church in 1918. In later life they bought a confectioner's shop in Olive Lane Darwen. While Alice looked after the shop and their three children, William continued working the night shift at Know Mill, travelling by train to Entwistle. William retired from the mill in 1949 aged 60, after 44 yrs service.

The tenancy of New House Farm eventually passed to Richard youngest son of George (senior) and Jane. After spending his early life just fifty yards from the railway track, it comes as no surprise that Richard took up work for the Lancashire and Yorkshire Railway as a porter and signalman. He married Alice Rigby, a weaver, in 1893. The railway company allowed all employees and their families free rail travel to anywhere in the British Isles and the Briggs family enjoyed many holidays in Ireland. After 16 years working for the railway, Richard Briggs then tried his hand at printing at Know Mill, and later as a butcher's assistant. Finally he and his growing family emigrated to Canada to seek a better life in Montreal and Richard died there in1959 aged 80.

Other than George Briggs (senior) who spent his working life at Lower House Farm and New House Farm, members of the Briggs and the Yates families moved about Entwistle with great rapidity, as befits tenants rather than farm owners. Other members of the family are found working as labourers in local industries including the Lancashire and Yorkshire Railway, Blackhill Brick, Know Mill, Round Barn Quarry and Bolton Water Works.

The following table is included to clarify the relationships between the main members of the Briggs family mentioned above.

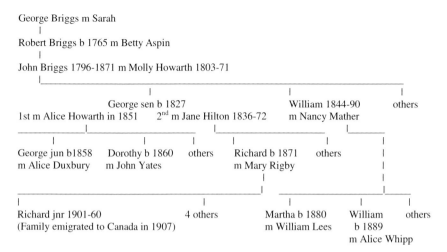

```
George Briggs m Sarah
   |
Robert Briggs b 1765 m Betty Aspin
   |
John Briggs 1796-1871 m Molly Howarth 1803-71
   |_____
                     |                              |              |
             George sen b 1827               William 1844-90     others
1st m Alice Howarth in 1851    2nd m Jane Hilton 1836-72    m Nancy Mather
_____|_____    |_____  |_____
   |             |          |        |                 |         |
George jun b1858  Dorothy b 1860  others   Richard b 1871  others  |
m Alice Duxbury   m John Yates            m Mary Rigby             |
                                                 |                 |
_____|   _____|_____
   |                              |              |           |         |
Richard jnr 1901-60            4 others    Martha b 1880   William   others
(Family emigrated to Canada in 1907)       m William Lees  b 1889
                                                          m Alice Whipp
```

Children born to the above families and surviving infancy are as follows:

To John and Molly: - James (b 1823), Jane (b 1825), George senior (b 1823), Peggy (b 1828, Mary (b 1830), Richard (b 1831), Sarah (b 1833), Martha (b1835), Ann (b1838), William (b 1844).

To George senior and Alice: - James (b 1856), George junior (b1858), Dorothy (b 1840), Martha (b 1863), Mary (b 1865).

To George senior and Jane: - John (b 1868), Thomas (b 1870), Richard (b 1871), Elizabeth (b 1872).

To William (1844-90) and Nancy (1846-1905): - John (b 1872), Thomas (b 1874), Sam (b 1876), Martha (b 1880), Mary (b 1882), William (b 1889).

To Richard and Mary: - John (1894-1978), George ?, Richard junior (1901-60), Minnie (1903-63), James (1906-1991).

William Briggs (1889-1955) from a pre 1914 photograph.

Marriage of William Briggs to Alice Whipp in 1918.

Marriage in 1903 of Samuel Briggs of Lower House Farm (1876-1933) to Alice Isherwood (b 1876) of Far Hillock Farm, Blacksnape.

Marriage of Martha Ann Briggs (1880-1954) to William Harold Lees (1876-1950) at St Anne's Church in 1906.

John Yates at Edge Fold Farm in 1915.

John and Dorothy Yates with their daughter in 1955.

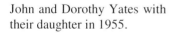

CHAPTER VI   ROADS AND SETTLEMENTS

6.1   ROADS

The Roman Road, originally built in the reign of Julius Agricola in AD 97, from Manchester to Ribchester, passes through Entwistle from south to north. This road was little more than a single horse track until it was rebuilt in the late eighteenth century and then only of real importance for a period of some 40 years before being displaced by a new turnpike. The present road is generally built on the foundations of the Roman Road but in places it deviates from the original but is no longer clearly visible, having been farmed over for centuries. In places it is some two feet below the surface, but in frosty weather or after a heavy snow fall the line and width of the road can be seen.

In 1775 the cost of repairing the old Blackburn Road was assessed at £52 10sh and a tax was levied on certain Entwistle residents to cover the expense as follows:

Name	Residence	Contribution		
		£	sh	d
John Entwistle	Lower House	3	13	0
Thomas Greenhalgh	Whittlestone Head	2	15	0
William Entwistle	The Edge	-	3	0
John Brandwood (sen)	New Hall	3	18	3
John Entwistle (sen)		-	16	0
Thomas Thomasson		1	5	0
James Brandwood, steward		3	1	0
Thomas Entwistle	Ramwells	2	5	0
John Entwistle (the younger)	Olden Fold	3	12	0
William Entwistle		-	15	0
Joseph Kay	Edge Foot Farm	1	15	0
Ralph Entwistle	Old Livings	3	12	0

By 1790 the road through Entwistle was still in an atrocious condition and building the new Bolton–Blackburn turnpike was being considered. However the old Roman Road was still important and in 1796 Blackburn parish advertised for tenders for the making up and renewing of various lengths between Blackburn and Bury. One successful tender was awarded to John Metcalf, a well known and respected road engineer from Knaresborough who was credited with completing many road projects in Lancashire and Yorkshire.

Blackburn Road, as the Roman Road is now called in Entwistle, is still the most useful of the highways that pass through the township. It passes by Wayoh Fold, Round Barn, Whittlestone Head and other important settlements. However it lost its importance as a through route when the Bolton to Blackburn Turnpike road (now A666) was authorized in 1797 and opened soon after. The new road does not actually enter Entwistle but runs along the western boundary.

The new turnpike accommodated through traffic between Manchester and Blackburn that previously passed through Entwistle, but otherwise did little for the township, to which it was connected only by a rough occupation road across Cranberry Moss and through Whittlestone Head. The main advantage of the road to Entwistle seems to have laid in the transportation of coal from Cranberry Moss Collieries down to Darwen and Turton. The only other connection to the turnpike was from Edge Fold and Edge Lane to a junction with the turnpike near the Duckworth Arms along New Meadows Road, but this is shown as a private road on the 1850 six inch OS map and the extent to which the public might use it in the years immediately after the turnpike was built is not clear.

The turnpike replaced the old Kings Highway from Bolton to Blackburn through Dimple and Bull Hill into Darwen. It was mostly built close to and parallel with the old highway and although an alternative route through part of Entwistle was considered, it was not adopted. Entwistle, already served by the Roman Road would not be expected to generate sufficient new traffic to attract the turnpike.

Other roads formerly of significance in the township include Lee lane which leaves the Roman Road near Wayoh Farm, climbs the north side of Broadhead valley, passes Naze End and Lower House farms and at one time provided a route over the hills to Haslingden. In the mid nineteenth century it acted as a haul road for coal from Broadhead Collieries.

Edge Lane, described later, is another old route that connected many of the properties in Entwistle with the outside world. It ran from Turton, past Entwistle Hall and other large properties, over Cranberry Moss and into Darwen.

Higher Cranberry Lane offered a route well used by mill workers and market traders in the 18th and 19th centuries. It ran from Grimehills on the Roman Road through Whittlestone Head Farm and Jacketmans Farm to join Lower Cranberry Lane near Sough, passing several coal mines on the way.

A final route known as Knowles Gutter ran from Whittlestone Head to a junction with Edge Lane at Ramwells. It was once part of an old drove route between Turton and Haslingden and is mentioned as an ancient highway in a deed of 1844 held by the Lancashire and Yorkshire Railway.

All the township roads were the responsibility of the highways surveyor and repairs were paid for from local taxes. Residents were legally obliged to spend a certain number of days each year on repairing the roads, known as 'statute labour' it was supposed to be one reason for the poor condition of many roads.

6.2   WHITTLESTONE HEAD

The hamlet of Whittlestone Head, adjacent to the Roman Road, may be as old as Entwistle itself, being first mentioned in a boundary deed in 1380. It is situated between the Manor of Entwistle and the Manor of Hoddlestone.

In the early Tyldesley papers published between 1555 and 1670 reference is made to a property known as the *'Widdlestone Tenement'*, which probably refers to *'Greenhalgh House'*, in the Hearth Tax return the home of Amos Greenhalgh. The property was later described as a farmhouse, built of coursed sandstone rubble with quoins, and a split stone flag roof with chimney stack close to the left gable with a two-bay baffle-entry plan and two low storeys.

In the Protestation Return for Entwistle, in 1642, no less than five Greenhalghs living at Whittlestone Tenement had signed: William, Arthur, Thurston, Richard and John, with a *'Thomas Grynaulghe'* (constable) as witness.

One of the feats of Victorian engineering (c.1840) started at Whittlestone Head when the 'Bolton, Darwen and Blackburn Railway' proposed to build the largest railway tunnel in the country, 1 mile 15 yards long, under Cranberry Moss.

The earliest recorded preacher in Entwistle was the Reverend Winder MA who was Curate of Bury Parish Church, 1767-1847, and Pastor at Edgworth Congregational Church, 1823-1846. He spent many years in Edgworth, Broadhead and Entwistle, giving religious instruction to the people in those isolated communities and started Sunday Schools at Whittlestone Head, Crow Trees and Broad Meadows. Most of his preachings were exercised from tiny cottages in Quarlton, Broadhead, Belmont, Egerton and Higher Crow Trees Farm, Entwistle. His congregation came in the main from farming stock, hand loom weavers, coal miners and children with no education. In 1822, a small chapel was built for him in Edgworth near Crown Point.

Having struggled for years to establish some kind of a school or chapel, Winder started a school on Sabbath days at Whittlestone Head in 1807 but it took another eighty years before a purpose built church was consecrated there. One can well imagine the scene on a Sunday afternoon as the Rev John Winder, resplendent on his horse, complete with Bible and cheese sandwiches in his saddlebag, rode into Whittlestone Head, with a backdrop reminiscent of a Wild West film to hold a service in a labourer's cottage. When hundreds of men and women on their day off from building the railway and money in their pockets were looking for more ale, it must have been a challenge for old Rev Winder.

Rev Winder died in 1847 and a tablet was erected in his memory in the Old Chapel by his two sons which read:

'To the memory of the late Rev. John Winder, obit 20th June, 1847, in his 80th year. His remains now lie in the body of this chapel. He was the first pastor of the congregation of Independents assembling in the neighbourhood and founder of this place of worship, among whom he laboured as a dutiful minister of Christ for upwards of 40 years and went to his grave in peace.'

Not until 1884/5 did religion take a firm hold in Whittlestone Head when a group of Christians formed a trust to set up a chapel. Mr John Barlow, the younger, of Crow Trees House who died in 1870, became the driving force behind a new Congregational Chapel for Whittlestone Head, on approximately 260 square yards of land. An indenture dated October 8th 1884 includes information on the conveyance of the buildings to be used as a Chapel, the Trust Deeds, the Schedule covering the form of worship, various Provisos and the signatories to the agreement.

The Indenture describes the building as an assigned cottage (a messuage or dwelling house with outbuildings and land) to be used for public worship according to the usages of Protestant Dissenters of the Congregational denomination commonly called Independents and being *'Phedo-Baptists'*. This was probably a misspelling of 'pseudo' although why Independents or Congregationalists should be so called is unclear. The chapel was situated on Lower Lane, an ancient way, running from Whittlestone Head down the east side of Whittlestone Brook, which it crossed at Clough Bottom Farm and then continued on past Know Mill to Hob Lane. The messuage was conveyed by a group of 17 local people to an elected body of trustees representing the congregation of members and communicants, known as the Society. The messuage was to be used regularly for assemblies to worship, for the instruction of children and adults, and for other religious and philanthropic purposes.

Some of the Society's seat holders paid pew-rents and gave or bequeathed monies to invest in Government Stock or real estate. Part of the interest received was given to those seatholders who paid pew rents; the other part was used to cover insurance against fire, payments to workmen for maintenance and repairs to the buildings and the upkeep and support of clergy and officers.

The Trust Deed only permitted those *'Phedo-Baptist'* Pastors who would hold, teach, preach and maintain the doctrines of Christian faith as set forth in the *'Agreed Schedule'*, the latter being a document which listed the strict doctrine and discipline of the Society, similar to the Calvinists' principles of belief. Any Pastor *'found or proved by reliable testimony of immoral conduct, or who shall cease to be of the "Phedo-Baptist" denomination, or shall preach any other doctrines not in harmony with the Agreed Schedule'* was to be removed from office if this was voted in favour and approved by the Members.

One of the several strict provisos in the Indenture was that the Society should have full power to manage all their financial and spiritual affairs including the admission, suspension and/or exclusion of members, and the election, suspension and dismissal of ministers, pastors, deacons and other officers.

The Trust Deed included a clause that if the Society be dissolved or dispersed and not be united again for six months, or if the approved form of worship be discontinued for two years or more, then the hereditaments must be directed to the Lancashire Independent College or the Lancashire Congregational Union or to the charge of pastors of other *'Phedo-Baptist'* churches.

There were twelve Trustees initially in 1884:

From Darwen: James Cocker, brush manufacturer; Thomas Thomason Greenwood, gent; Thomas Shorrock, weaver; John Brotherton, quarryman.
From Edgworth: John Nelson, shoemaker; Joseph Rothwell, warehouseman; Thomas Marsden, joiner; Walter Whitehead, coal merchant.
From Entwistle: John MacVine, gent; Edmund Entwistle, farmer; Joseph Down, quarryman.

By 1908, mainly due to deaths, only three of the original Trustees remained: Edmund Entwistle, Joseph Rothwell and John Brotherton. They were joined by eight newly appointed people, thus restoring the total number of Trustees to twelve in September 19th 1908 as follows:

From Darwen: William Hitchin, gent; Samuel Morris, labourer; William Shorrock Heap, weaver; William Henry Marsden, farmer; James Brotherton, weaver; John Edwin Holden, grocer; Frederick Tyson, carter.
From Entwistle: Samuel Bright Nightingale, farmer.

The chapel closed in 1946 and later was used, for a while, to house poultry.

Former Congregational Chapel (1885-1946) at Whittlestone Head.
Now converted to a private home.

Foundation stone in the former Whittlestone Head Congregational Chapel.

Tavern Farm, Whittlestone Head; situated on the banks of Whittlestone Head Brook, the building was used as a tripe works in the 1840s

Railway Tavern, at the rear of the above Tavern Farm, c1910.

Lower Whittlestone Head Farm, formerly Greenhalgh's, built in the 1600s.

Whittlestone Head from Round Barn Quarry: note the tunnel ventilating shaft on Cranberry Moss.

Top o'th' Meadows Farm, Grimehills, which has a 1783 datestone.

Hay time at Top o'th' Meadows Farm in 1945 with
Alf Dixon, John Dixon, Jack Lewis and Sid Green.

Pike House Barn on the Roman Road (Blackburn Road) in 2010.

Pike House with datestone RAB 1740 (Roger & Anne Brandwood), in 1975.

6.3   ROUND BARN

Turnpike House, or Pike House, with its date stone engraved RAB 1740, was built by the Brandwood family adjacent to the Roman Road and less than a hundred yards from Round Barn Quarry. The building is in coursed watershot thin sandstone, like that occurring at the nearby quarry, with large quoins, gable copings, and kneelers; originally it had a flagstone roof with gable chimneys.

It is quite possible that the first quarrying at Round Barn was done by the Brandwoods some time in the late 17th century, but there is no clear evidence. However the first Ordnance Survey map indicates that by 1847 the quarry was established and that a little community had evolved around Round Barn. Construction of the railway no doubt made greater demands on the quarry.

With well over three thousand workers (mainly Irish) living and working at Whittlestone Head for over three years while Sough Tunnel was being built, it is not surprising that four public houses within a short distance of each other did a splendid trade. There was the Railway Tavern at Whittlestone Head, the Crown and Thistle at Grimehills Bridge, the Moscrop Inn at Middle Aushaw and the Wellington Inn at Round Barn.

In 1847 John Fish was the landlord at the Wellington Inn and from 1871 to 1881, a Mr John Lowe and his wife Esther plus their seven children were living there. Next door to the Wellington Inn in an attached building was the Entwistle Workhouse.

By 1847, eight cottages had been built at Round Barn together with two large dormitories for quarry workers, called locally the 'House of Lords' and 'House of Commons'. The 'House of Lords', which was the top row, cost one penny per night and the 'House of Commons', the lower row, cost one halfpenny per night.

Irish migrants continued to live near the quarry and in 1881 fifteen employees had been born in Ireland, young men in their twenties and still unmarried. The population of Entwistle at that time was 555; most were employed in farming, at Know Mill, on the railway, or in the quarries. In the Census of 1881 farms and cottages were recorded as lying empty as was the Union School at Whittlestone Head. Perhaps hard times had arrived in Entwistle.

When the quarry declined and finally closed, in the mid 1920s, the residents of Round Barn were in the most desperate of circumstances with little or no work. Many people were near starvation.

The Institute in Edgworth, endowed by the Barlow family of mill owners, seems to have been instrumental in providing some relief to the needy, through its manager William Kingsley. The following documents now preserved in the Institute's records give some idea of the circumstances at Round Barn.

To Mr Kingsley, Village Institute   Dear Sir
I am troubling you again. I have heard of a case this morning at Roundbarn. Mrs McGuire's little boy is unable to come to school having no clogs or stockings.
She has sent a note to Mr Williams saying 'through slack time at the Roundbarn Quarry' she has been unable to get clogs at all. We have had a pair sent but they are too small – they measure 7 inches – she wants a size larger. Can anything be done about the matter.
Yours truly
L Taylor, Headmistress, Hob Lane Council School, Edgworth: 1925

To Mr R H Whitehead, Treasurer, Turton & Edgworth Guild of Help   Dear Sir
I herewith enclose you a cheque for Two Pounds for the Guild of Help Funds from our Employee's Benevolent Fund. Trusting that you will kindly acknowledge same in due course and oblige.
Yours truly
Pro The Works Committee, The Know Mill Printing Co, Entwistle.   13 August 1925

To Mr Kingsley, Village Institute   Dear Sir
Please find 3sh 9d that has been collected. Mrs W McLeary is a very deserving case. Her husband cannot work and there is only one worker. There are six children.
Yours truly
L Taylor, Green Alders Cottage, Edgworth   1925

To Mr Allen, Village Institute   Dear Mr Allen
Just a few lines on behalf of Mrs Rimmington, she is almost starving and has been all winter, she has only got one day's work (on Monday) and that is for rent. And ½ day on Saturday for coal, nothing for food only depending on what the neighbours give her, things have got so bad with us all we cannot afford a meal, as the quarry has been slack for months.
Hoping Mr Allen you will see into her distress at once, besides she is one of your country women, not a foreigner, she is a clean, decent, hard-working woman. You can make all enquires and you will find what I tell you is true.
I remain Dear Sir, Yours truly,
A McGuire, Round Barn Cottages: 25 January 1926

To Mr Kingsley, Village Institute   Dear Sir
I have just heard that Mrs Rimmington of Round Barn Cottages is in want of a little help. She has only 4 shillings a week coming in for washing and that is all she has. I thought I would let you know as soon as possible.
Yours truly
L Taylor, Hob Lane Council School: 26 January 1926.

To Mrs Taylor, Village Institute   Dear Mrs Taylor
I have written to Mr Allen about Mrs Rimmington. She has only got one day's work and takes that to pay her rent. Since I explained to Mr Allen she has got some food from Isherwood's. She is very thankful, but wants coal as well as food. Mr Hayward told me to refer her to you. Hoping you will do your best for her, she is a deserving case.
Yours truly
Annie McGuire: 29 January 1926

To Mrs Taylor,Village Institute   Dear Mrs Taylor
Just a few lines on behalf of Mrs Rimmington she is very thankful for the coal you got sent to her. When I wrote to Mr Allen some time ago about her distress, he told me she should have been seen to e'er then, now then Isherwoods sent her some food twice since only, and they told her it was only temporary. Mr Allen told her to see you about this. So will you please see she gets a bit of fresh food every week. Bread a fortnight old is not so nice to eat, a small bit and get it weekly would be better. They sent her only one quarter of bacon altogether, I know you will see things made right, when you have time.
You know her, and you understand better than strangers.
Yours truly
A McGuire, Round Barn Cottages: 1926.

To Mr Kingsley, Village Institute   Dear Mr Kingsley
I received the enclosed this morning from Mrs McGuire. Perhaps Mr Allen may know something of the case.
Yours truly
L Taylor Hob Lane Council School, Edgworth   4 February 1926

Mr Kingsley, Village Institute   Dear Mr Kingsley
Please find enclosed a letter which I have received from Mrs McGuire, you will see it is about Mrs Rimmington's case.
Yours truly
L Taylor, Hob Lane Council School: 1926

Mr Kingsley, Village Institute   Dear Sir
I received your letter this morning. In regard to the boy's clogs, Mrs McGuire bought him a pair of shoes this weekend and he is now coming to school. In Mrs Rimmington's case I think she is wanting help for a length of time, she ought to apply to the Guardians. In her case I think Mrs McGuire's letter was altogether bad form.
I am your truly
L Taylor, Hob Lane Council School: 22 March 1926

The following are copies of orders for provisions submitted to local retailers by the Barlow Institute for those receiving support:

Turton, Edgworth Guild of Help, Village Institute.
To Edgworth Stores
Please supply Mrs Thos Fish of Broadhead Road with 10 shillings worth of provisions each week for two weeks and debit the same.
W Kingsley, Hon Sec   16 August 1926

50

Guild of Help
To J Isherwood Ltd
Groceries 6 shillings: Mrs Rimmington, Round Barn   19 October 1926

Guild of Help
Please supply one quart of milk to Mrs Smith – Isherwood Fold each morning for three weeks, to begin on 17 February and then give me a bill for the same.
Yours faithfully
W Kingsley   16 February 1927

Below are records of accounts submitted for payment to the Barlow Institute, for goods and services received by the needy.

To Turton and Edgworth Guild of Help, Village Institute
Bought of A Mellody, Grocery and Provision Dealer, 76 High Street, Turton,
10 shillings
A McGuire   16 January 1926

To Turton Guild of Help
J Isherwood Ltd, 8 & 10 Bentley Row, Edgworth, Grocers, Corn, Flour and Provision Merchants   6 shillings
Mrs Rimmington, Round Barn   28 January 1926

To Turton Guild of Help
J Isherwood Ltd, Grocers, Corn, Flour and Provisions Merchants   6 shillings
Mrs Rimmington   3 February 1926

To The Village Institute

2pr sole & heel	@ 4sh 6d	9-0
2pr heel	@ 1sh 2d	2-4
1pr child's heel	@ 10d	0-10
2pr new clogs	@ 7sh 6d	15-0
1pr boots clogged	@ 1sh 9d	1-9
1 pr clogs clogged	@ 1sh 9d	1-9
1 pr clogged & ironed	@ 2sh 2d	2-2
1 tin polish	3d	0-3
Irons	3sh 2d	3-2
		£1-16-3

Mrs Whittaker   Feb 1926

Paid W K [William Kingsley]

Round Barn Cottages, formerly accommodation for quarrymen.

Round Barn Quarry Cottages at Walton Fold on Blackburn Road.

Round Barn: on the left was the Entwistle Workhouse and right was the former Duke of Wellington Inn.

Rear view of former workhouse and Wellington Inn.

6.4   CHETHAM TRUST AND THE WORKHOUSES

Before the Poor Law Amendment Act of 1834, each township was responsible for its poor which is why Entwistle had its own workhouse at Round Barn. In 1841 Thomas Briggs and Jas Mather were the Overseers of the Entwistle Poor and by 1847 many Entwistle people had found themselves in the Round Barn workhouse due mainly to ill health, old age or shortage of employment. A small selection of these included Richard Whitehead (Whittlestone Head) aged 53 years, a weaver and single (described as *'difficult'*) who had found that a cottage hand loom weaver could not compete with factory looms. Others were described as Jas Booth, (63) weaver *'soft'*; Jas Lomax, (81) *'old aged'*; Rachel Whitehead, (82) widow, *'old age'*; Mary Holding, (48) weaver, single *'difficult'*; Ralph Entwistle, (47) weaver, *'soft'*; Jacob Wood, widower (30) *'sick'*.

Entwistle Workhouse was not the only provision made for the poor. In 1748 the trustees of Humphrey Chetham Esq made an agreement to rent, for three lives of 31 years, the farmhouse and land in Turton known as Goose Cote Hill comprising a house, barn, outbuildings, orchard, paddocks, meadows and fields of about 40 acres with the aim of building a workhouse for the poor of Turton, Edgworth, Quarlton, and Entwistle. The new house cost £64-7s-9d and was large enough to house 60 people. By 1820 the workhouse housed 138 poor souls and was so overcrowded, despite extension work finished in 1825, that it was extended again between 1826 and 1827 in a period of great unemployment. Eventually all the inmates of the Entwistle Workhouse were transferred to Goose Cote Hill and, after 1861, to the Bolton Union Workhouse at Fishpool.

The workhouse, financed by the Chetham Trust, spent much time and money on the poor of Entwistle and Turton. It helped the able-bodied to adjust to the industrial changes and taught fresh skills before placing men into new jobs.

The Turton Poor Book of the Chetham Trust dated 1794-1822, plus the New Book dated 1823-1856 give a graphic insight into the plight of some of the poor from Entwistle. Each year the Trust distributed linen cloth to those in desperate need of clothing. A random sample reads:

'Wm Mayoh of Entwissl (Weaver) family of 8, received cloth for a period of 6 years, 1828 – 7yds, 1829 – 7yds, 1830 – 8yds (now 7 children), 1831 – 7yds, 1832 – 7 ½ yds, 1833 – 12 ½ yds'.
'Robt Howarth, Entwissl (labourer) 8 children, 1833 – 12 ½ yds, Decd'.
Ann Mayoh (Widower, Weaver of Overhouses) 1828 – 6yds'.
'Elizabeth Kay "Edgfold", 5yds cloth May 30th 1833'.
'Wm Mayoh Snr. 8yds, June 1830'.
'Mrs Wm Mayoh 4yds 1828'.

6.5   WAYOH FOLD

In 1670 during the sale of the Tyldesleys' Entwistle Estate a new development, Wayoh Fold, came onto the market. The Fold, built c1600, stands alongside the ancient highway, Blackburn Road, and was traditionally home to the village blacksmith. Sitting on a high prominence above Wayoh Bridge it comprised a farmhouse, barn, cow byre, stables, two cottages and a blacksmith's shop. Without doubt the most important tradesman in a township in centuries past was the blacksmith; for fixing, making, repairing, sharpening or shoeing he was the man to see.

John Sharples worked as the blacksmith and machine repairer at Bromley Cross Stone Quarries which closed down in 1911. Within days Mr Sharples moved his family to No 4 Round Barn Cottages. He spent the next 15 years as Blacksmith at Round Barn Quarry and was engaged in all manner of metal work, fabrication, sharpening tools and repairs.

In 1925 Round Barn Quarry, along with various cottages, farms and barns, was put up for sale. Mr R Brooks, a businessman and a relative of John Sharples, bought a substantial part of this property and proceeded to resell some cottages and farms to local families. John Sharples purchased the nearby Wayoh Fold for £600 and re-established the former blacksmith's shop. There was much trade from the local farming community for a skilled smith and in a very short time he had established other blacksmith's shops in Edgworth behind The White Horse Inn, at Turton Bottoms behind the Spread Eagle Inn and in the village of Chapeltown. He was ably assisted by his son James as an apprentice blacksmith. During the Second World War John Sharples, who died in 1947, was employed at Know Mill maintaining the machinery.

In 1938 James Sharples, then 21, was employed as a farrier for Aspin Brothers at the Duke of York forge in Blackburn. He travelled to and from work by train, returned to the farm in time for evening milking and spent weekends at his father's blacksmith shop working on farm machinery. James spent his later life shoeing shire horses for Thwaites and Co., Brewers of Blackburn. He retired after 23 years service in 1983.

The Wayoh Fold cottages became quite a popular holiday resort between the 1920s and 50s for the people of Darwen, Bolton and Blackburn. Many of them spent their week's break in comfortable caravans spaced about the gardens and grounds. The proprietors, Mrs Pomfret and later Mrs Emily Chamberlin, made a very good living catering for them.

Wayoh Fold in 2000.

Wayoh Fold, barn and cowhouse, originally built c1600.

Wayoh Fold Cottages and 'tea rooms', 1930s.

Remains of Naze End Farm on Lee Lane.

Clive and Colin
Timms at
Wayoh Fold
Farm, 1930s.

Young James
Sharples of
Wayoh Fold, late
1920s.

James Sharples
with
'blacksmith'
Jack Sharples.

Jim Sharples, blacksmith.

Sharples family wedding party at Wayoh Fold in 1941.

Sandra Foster at Wayoh Fold, 1950.

Hilda and Sandra Foster at Wayoh Tea Room, 1950.

The McCreary and McGuire families at Wayoh Tea Rooms, 1930s.

The McCreary and McGuire sisters at Round Barn c1939.

Wedding of Pat Hatzar and Elizabeth McCreary of Round Barn, c1939.

6.6.   EDGE LANE

The Edge or Edg (sic) Road was described as an *'Ancient Highway'* in a deed dated 1603 in the Tyldesley papers. It is worthy of note that this road, which runs through Chapeltown village, Overshores, Armsgrove, Entwistle Hall and continues straight through the middle of Entwistle Township, from east to west, was described as the *'King's Highway'*. The road served the most ancient halls and farmhouses in Entwistle: Higher Crow Trees built c.1700, Lower Crow Trees c.1250, Entwistle Hall c.1200, rebuilt 1500s, Entwistle New Hall 1695, Whitacars Farm 1594, Whittakers 1689, Edge Fold House 1590, Edge Farm c.1600, Edge Foot c.1450, rebuilt 1889, Castle Inn 1700s, Ramwells Farm 1610, Higher Boltons 1787, and Bannister House (described in a deed of 1487 as Bannister Hall).

In 1848, at the completion of the railway through Entwistle, Edge Road was diverted from Entwistle New Hall in an easterly direction away from Entwistle Old Hall. A new road originally named Entwistle Hall Lane, now Crow Trees Lane, was constructed on the north side of the Old Hall, which led past Higher Crow Trees house and Lower Crows Trees house. This road, which circumnavigated Know Mill Printworks and joined onto Hob Lane, suffered a massive land slip in 1895 which resulted in it being rerouted through the mill yard on Know Mill property. The old route was not reinstated until after the demolition of Know Mill in the 1950s.

In 1938 the residents and owners of Entwistle New Hall, Mr and Mrs John Blair, petitioned Turton District Council for the repair and upkeep of Edge Lane, which ran from the railway bridge at the boundary of their property, along the west side of the Hall, over Cranberry Moss and down into Darwen. Turton Council refused, until the Blairs' legal counsel did some in-depth research into the history of the Edge Road. It soon became clear that this road was in daily use by a Mr Kay as far back as 1635 and was mentioned in connection with a lease of part of Entwistle Hall to the same gentleman. The new tenant was authorized *'to pass on horseback or on foot, with carts or carriages or drifts of cattle along Edge Road and back to the Hall'*. Turton Council at last consented to the request in 1938 and redrained and resurfaced the road from New Hall to Edge Fold House.

New Hall, Edge Lane.

Edge Lane and New Hall Farm looking towards the railway station.

The two Bridge Cottages, now adjoining the Strawbury Duck Inn.

The front garden at Lower Crow Trees, just before demolition in the 1950s.

Higher Crow Trees Farm.

Door overmantle from Whitakers Barn Farm set in the wall on Edge Lane.

Edge Lane: the wall on the left contains the overmantle shown above.

Holly Bank House.

Holly Bank Cottages in 2011.

CHAPTER VII KNOW MILL AND TEXTILES

7.1   TEXTILES

In most farms and cottages, before the Industrial Revolution, the women would spin the wool from local sheep and later imported cotton, while the men would weave the product on simple hand looms. They produced more than needed for themselves and were able to sell off the excess which brought in a cash income, often necessary to supplement the meagre returns from agriculture in this upland district.

In the very early days a chapman (packman) would call at each farmhouse, pay for the finished cloth and leave more raw cotton or wool as required. In the late eighteenth century, people of Entwistle would take their finished cloth to the Green Man public house on Green Arms Road to sell and buy in raw wool or cotton, from a cloth dealer who would be there for the day once a fortnight. By the nineteenth century such hand loom weavers as remained generally took their cloth to the 'Cotton Exchange' in Cranberry Fold across the township boundary in Darwen. It is said that it was common practice for the young ladies of the district to hire or borrow a donkey for the day to carry cotton goods to the exchange. They travelled in twos and threes through Whittlestone Head along Higher Cranberry Lane, over the Cranberry Moss and down to Cranberry Fold where the cloth would be inspected by the 'taker-in' and paid for. This would be a distance of about three miles from Entwistle. After selling their cloth there were reports of people being robbed on the way home.

Until the early nineteenth century hand loom weaving offered a reasonable means for a man to make a living. However through competition from increasingly sophisticated machinery in weaving sheds the trade gradually deteriorated until it became ill paid and pauper creating. Some of the weavers might have as many as five hand looms in special loomshops in their cottages but they still could not compete with the mills, where eventually most of them were forced to work to make a living.

The gradual extinction of the cottage textile industry in Entwistle caused much hardship, especially as no spinning or weaving mills ever seem to have been established to provide alternative employment.

However the presence of copious river water did promote the establishment of another branch of the textile industry, bleaching, which eventually was to become of great importance to Entwistle.

7.2   ENTWISTLE CORN MILL

The corn mill for the Manor of Entwistle, complete with a water wheel was situated at the bottom of Hob Lane at the meeting of Whittlestone Head and Broadhead Brooks. The area was known as 'Knowles Farm' and included 35 acres of land. The mill had been owned by the Lord of the Manor from medieval times until 1761 when it came into the ownership of Christopher Baron and then passed to his son Roger Baron who, in 1776, was living in part of the Old Hall until he died in 1785, after apparently becoming bankrupt. The subsequent disposal of the corn mill led to the development of Know Mill.

7.3   CALICO PRINTING IN ENTWISTLE

Perhaps the most significant thing to happen in Entwistle from a resident's point of view, started with a small advertisement that appeared in the 'Manchester Mercury' on 28th June 1785 which read:

'By order of Mr Roger Baron, (a bankrupt) of Entwistle: To be sold, a farm or tenement, situated in Entwistle, county of Lancs called Know Mill, consisting of a dwelling house with suitable outbuildings and 35 acres of land in the occupation of Richard Bently and of a Corn mill, supplied with such a stream of water (Whittlestonehead Brook and Broadhead Brook) *that would extremely easily be converted to the purposes of carding or spinning cotton or linen goods, together with a kiln appertaining to such mill.'*

That, doubtless, was the first faltering step of the 'Know Mill Calico Printing Co.' By the early 19th century it had developed into a bleach works as was shown by a further advertisement in the 'Manchester Mercury' of 16th Feb 1802:

'To be let for any term of years and entered on in April a Bleaching Croft called "Knowles Mill" situated in Entwistle 6 miles from Bolton, and 8 miles from Blackburn, containing a large dwelling house, 2 small houses, a barn, stable, bowkhouse, dressing house and 2 dry houses. Eighty yards long with all suitable fixtures for the bleaching business. For further particulars apply at No 33 Cannon Street, Manchester, or at John Chaster Printworks, Edgworth. N.B. Plenty of brook or spring water'.

The mill continued to grow and change hands as the same newspaper reported on 26th Jan 1813:

'To Printers and Bleachers etc Sale by auction by Mr Mansell at the house of Wm. Wood, Bulls Head Inn, Turton, Nr Bolton on Wed 17th Feb, 1813, at 3

o'clock in the aft (unless previously disposed of by private contract of which timely notice will be given). A desirable freehold estate of inheritance, called or known by the name of "Know Mill" now used as a bleaching croft situated in Entwistle near Turton, 6 miles Bolton, 8 miles Blackburn, 17 miles Manchester, comprising a large double house, five rooms on a floor, 5 cottages, barn, stable and shippons, 3 stone erections of buildings 2 storeys high used as bowkhouse, dressing house and store rooms, 80 yards of dry housing, together with several closes and parcels of good arable meadow and pasture land containing 3 acres of the large Cheshire measure or thereabouts. The croft is let to Mr John Blechley as a tenant at will and is supplied with a brook or spring water. The spring will fill a 3 inch bore nearly all the year, coal may be had in the immediate neighbourhood'. (The sale was postponed until 3 March).

It would seem that Know Mill led a very precarious existence as by December 1815 the property was once again for sale, still in the hands of Mr Blechley.

7.4   THE PROSPEROUS YEARS

By 1840 the mill was well established and in the capable hands of Messrs Roxbury, Ashworth & Co. They were listed in 'English Calico Printers', March 1841, as having 40 printing tables, which suggests quite an expanding firm. The industrial power to drive the mill was one water wheel producing approximately 12 horsepower.

1861 saw Mr John Burford & Sons controlling the works then called 'Know Mill Calico Printers', but by 1864 the property was actually owned by the Rostron family. Mrs Sarah Ann Rostron of Sandy Bank, Edgworth leased the factory to George Holt as manager. In the Bolton Improvement Act of 1864, Item No. 61 says *'for the protection of the land and premises known as Know Mill Printworks in the occupation of Mr George Holt – to the provision of new settling tanks and ponds etc, plans passed.'*

Considerable expansion then took place including a new bleach house erected in 1868, a large chimney built in 1872, about 150 feet high, and the boiler room was greatly extended. From this time, the corn mill and water wheel cease to be mentioned in the accounts. In 1878 a machine room and a new stable block were erected and it would seem that this large expense overstretched their finances as the firm soon after became insolvent.

In 1878 the Bolton Guardian of Nov 23rd reported that Messrs Richard Wardman and Mr James MacAdam had filed for bankruptcy with liabilities of £56,000, although the Rostron family still owned all the property.

Calico printing in 1835.

A typical Lancashire print shop.

In the High Court of Justice,

CHANCERY DIVISION.

Mr. Justice Swinfen Eady.

Between THE MAYOR, ALDERMEN, AND
BURGESSES OF THE BOROUGH
OF BOLTON - - - - - Plaintiffs

and

THE KNOW MILL PRINTING
COMPANY LIMITED - - - Defendants.

ANSWERS TO INTERROGATORIES.

THE ANSWER of William Simpson the Chairman of Directors of the above named Defendant Company to the Interrogatories for his examination by the above named Plaintiffs.

IN ANSWER to the said Interrogatories I the above named William Simpson do solemnly and sincerely affirm as follows:—

1. IN ANSWER to the first of the said Interrogatories I say that some time between 1864 and 1872 a Bleach House was erected. In 1872 the present Chimney was erected. In 1878 a Machine Room and Stables were erected. In 1880 part of the present Colour House, the Blacksmith Shop, Mechanics Shop and Joiners Shop were built. In 1881 part of the present Boiler House was erected. In 1884 a Block Printing Shop, Roller Room and Drug Store Room were erected and the Boiler House was extended. In 1891 or 1892 a Packing Room, Preparing Room, and White Cloth Room were built. In 1893 there was a further extension of the Boiler House. In 1894 the Machine Room and old Stenter Room were erected the Colour Shop was extended and an Economiser Plant was erected. In 1895 the Time Office was erected. In 1896 the Effluent Treatment Plant was put down. In 1899 the Workpeople's Dining Room was built and in 1900 the new Dye House was erected in substitution for the old Dye House then existing and an Artesian Well was sunk and Pump Station erected. Save as hereinbefore mentioned the Know Mill Printing Works have not since the 14th of July 1864 the date of the passing of the Bolton Improvement Act 1864 been in any manner enlarged or extended.

Court proceedings recording the growth of Know Mill.

Distant view of Know Mill Print Works.

Sir Herbert Samuel, prospective Liberal candidate
with employees at Know Mill in 1935.

From 1880, under a new company, expansion continued and in 1881 the boiler house was extended to almost double its former size. In 1884 a new block printing shop, a roller room and drug store room were erected and the boiler room was again extended. In 1891/2 a packing room, preparing room and a new white cloth room were built. In 1893 there was a further extension to the boiler house. In 1894 there was more investment, the workforce increased, and a new machine and starter rooms were erected. The colour shop was extended and an 'Economiser Plant' was installed. By now the workforce had increased to over three hundred, requiring a time office to be built in 1895. More improvements followed and in 1896 the effluent treatment plant was built to stop chemical waste from polluting Wayoh reservoir.

In 1899 a new dining room and kitchens were built and in 1900 the new dye house was erected to replace the old one. An artesian well was sunk and a new pumping station completed. Bleaching and printing in such a large works required copious amounts of water to maintain production and there never seemed to be enough clean water. The firm received numerous letters of complaint from the Bolton Borough Water Department about polluting Whittlestone Head Brook which then passed straight into the Wayoh reservoir.

In 1902 there were more complaints from Bolton Borough Water Dept. and this time Mr William Simpson, Chairman of Directors of the Know Mill Printing Company Ltd, ended up in the High Court in Manchester (see court notice), but by now Know Mill had become part of the Bleachers' Association.

During the 1914-18 War orders came from the Government which meant full employment at Know Mill. The workforce exceeded 600 and 12 hour shifts were worked by day and night. This was the mill's most prosperous time. However, complaints and problems still occurred with Bolton Water Department, which were never to be resolved.

During all this expansion from the 1860s right through into the 1920s the Rostron family still retained ownership of all the land and the mill property, with leases granted to the various mill operators for a set period of years. By 1924 the lease on the Know Mill property was due to expire and the Bleachers' Association expended a great deal of time and effort negotiating for the purchase of Know Mill from the trustees of the late Mrs Sarah Ann Rostron. The trustees were Messrs M Keith of Edgworth, William Woodcock, solicitor of Haslingden and F Whowell of Croich Hey, Tottington.

It was reported in the Bolton Evening News 5th Sept 1924: *'Know Mill Negotiations for Sale: It has been known for some time that Know Mill Printing Co. Ltd. intended to transfer the whole of their Entwistle business to their works at Walmersley, near Bury (Bevis Green) when their lease on the Know Mill property expires. For this purpose the company have been extending their Bury works and the 600 or 700 work people employed at Know Mill have been greatly concerned about their future. All kinds of rumours have been in circulation in the villages of Turton, Edgworth and Entwistle, a large proportion of whose residents depend upon the mill, and it will be agreeable news to them to learn that negotiations are at present proceeding for the purchase of the mill.*

Know Mill, which is let on a lease to the printing company is one of the finest and most prosperous concerns in the north. It has been working night and day for the past 40 years and it is inconceivable that such a place should close. Whether the new owners will carry on its present business or whether some other work will be set on foot is not yet known.'

This was not the death knell of Know Mill by any means though a shadow was cast by the proximity of Wayoh reservoir. One can imagine how much waste and slurry was being produced by a factory with 700 people working day and night. Bolton Water Dept made numerous complaints about water discolouration and the mill owners spent a considerable amount of money on filtration plant and new settlement beds, which improved matters somewhat but there was nevertheless a continuing problem.

The 1920s and 30s saw a steep downturn in orders in the bleaching and printing industry. Much of the work at Know Mill was transferred to Bevis Green, Bury and the workforce dwindled to near 200. There was a temporary improvement during the war years but the 1950s changed everything when the Wayoh reservoir, previously a compensation reservoir, began supplying clean drinking water to the people of Bolton. In 1953 plans were announced in Bolton that the Wayoh reservoir would be raised by 20 feet and as Know Mill stood level with the top water mark of the reservoir it was clear that the mill would have to go.

7.5   KNOW MILL AUCTION AND SALE

In 1958 the following article appeared in the Bolton Evening News:

'And so after over 150 years of industry and of being host to several generations of Entwistle people the mill finally closed its doors. The centre of village life, the hub of the community, the place where friendships were forged, where social events, and bowls, cricket, football matches were organized, where parties were held and dances arranged. Some local folk spent their entire working life at Know Mill.'

'Due to be demolished ahead of a new scheme to raise the Wayoh reservoir by 20 feet, a two day auction has been arranged for Tuesday and Wednesday next week. At the auction, held in the old "dye house" with its stone flagged floor and whitewashed walls, over 150 bidders, businessmen, dealers and private bidders gathered, all looking for a bargain, with over 750 lots on offer, including old and new machines some dismantled, sacks of nuts and bolts, complete buildings, wooden beams, Lancashire boilers, tables, chairs, office equipment etc'.

'Among the large crowds gathered there was a small group of old employees sadly wandering through the old works, doubtless remembering the good old days. These men had spent their entire working lives at the mill. Every machine sold, every piece of equipment knocked down for scrap was for them a tragic waste and a personal tragedy. They came to witness the mill's final hours and reflect on the times when almost all of the village of Entwistle worked there, men like Mr James Brooks of Bolton Road, Edgworth who had done 58 years service as foreman in one of the mill departments. He was almost overcome by emotion as he toured the mill for the last time. "It's a great tragedy" he said, as he stopped to find his workshop in ruins. "They were a good firm to work for and the old mill's become a part of village life that I'm going to find hard to lose. It's like losing a part of yourself after so many years."

Mr W Mather, the general manager of Know Mill Printing Company, said that when the mill was closed, all the people employed from the village had been given jobs at the company's other mill at Bevis Green Works near Bury. "It's a great pity that the history had to end here" he said, "but we shall do our best to carry it on at our other works. There is still some sentimentality in business, for instance the brass bell in the clock tower, the fire chief's helmet, over a hundred years old and worn by successive fire chiefs at the mill, and the old factory hooter which called the local employees to work, will not be sold but will be removed to our Bevis Green factory, as will the old cornerstone bearing the date 1834 taken from the old Print Shop which will be incorporated into another building at the Bury works."

After the auction took place the mill was demolished. Few workers chose to transfer to Bevis Green, Bury. The Wayoh reservoir was raised 20 feet and the old mill site was lost for ever.

By 1954 the number of cars registered in Entwistle had risen from 3 in 1939 to 20 and in that year a new public road was built to link Entwistle Station with Hob Lane and avoid the site of Know Mill. The previous road from Hob lane had gone through the mill yard to meet up with Entwistle Hall Lane. Turton Council tried to recover the cost (£4120) from the Entwistle residents but after much acrimonious discussion the charge was levied on the rates.

Know Mill, 1950s.

Roller-printer at Know Mill.

Know Mill: the loading bay.

Know Mill: the dye house.

Know Mill: Mrs Dorothy Fernley at the main entrance.

Know Mill: manager's house, built in 1928.

MANCHESTER OFFICE:
30, PRINCESS STREET,
MANCHESTER, 1.
TELEPHONE: CENTRAL 3277.

TELEGRAMS: "HARDCASTLE, BRADSHAW."
TELEPHONE: EAGLEY 21, 22 & 23.
STATION: BROMLEY CROSS.

LONDON OFFICE
HANOVER COURT,
HANOVER SQUARE, W.1.
TELEPHONE: MAYFAIR 3391.

THE JAMES HARDCASTLE KNOW MILL PRINTING COMPANY LTD.

CALICO PRINTERS DYERS & BLEACHERS

BRADSHAW WORKS,
BRADSHAW,
BOLTON............................

Miss. E. Hilton

Please quote:—

　　　　As a consequence of the decision of the Board of Management of the Bleachers' Association to close the Works, it is regretted that we have to terminate your employment with us on the 2nd August, 1963.

　　　　We wish to express our appreciaton of the loyal and faithful service you have given to the Company and to wish you every success in the future.

S. A. Granville

Know Mill: under demolition.

CHAPTER VIII   RESERVOIRS

8.1   BUILDING ENTWISTLE RESERVOIR

Entwistle is dominated by the reservoir built in 1832/36, which has a top water area of 94 acres and when full contains 760 million gallons of water. In comparison, Wayoh and Jumbles reservoirs contain 1,250 and 762 million gallons respectively.

An early dam at Belmont was constructed about 1827 by the Great and Little Bolton Waterworks Company. It was intended to take water from Eagley Brook for drinking purposes and provided a minimum supply of compensation water for the mills further downstream. Because of its success in regulating the flow of the water, other local mill owners began to build dams.

In 1831 moves were made towards building a reservoir at Entwistle. A meeting of owners and occupiers of mills and 'falls of water' along the rivers between Entwistle and Warrington was held at Haywards Hotel, Manchester on the 23rd August. They considered making and maintaining a reservoir in the townships of Turton and Entwistle to provide a more regular and constant supply of water. They were not interested in providing drinking water; the venture was purely a commercial undertaking to serve the new industries which had sprung up in the area. It was to be financed by *'an annual rate upon each occupier of fall'*. Falls were sections of the river which serviced individual mills for power or process water.

In 1832 Mr Thomas Ashworth was *'the engineer and agent to the said Commissioners.'* Ashworth's plan for the reservoir construction and the capital required to complete the project was simple and thorough: *'With the embankment at the said height put at 108 feet the entire reservoir will cost £16,941 13s. 4d.'* He suggested that all work should be done by *'loose and unsigned contracts consisting only of a written tender by the man or gangs of men (or women) for the rate of price at which he or they will perform certain work, this is best in a variety of small contracts. The work will be under the control of the surveyor* (Mr Ashworth). *Nor will the surveyor be obliged to continue him in work if his conduct is not satisfactory'*. Thus if the snow, or frost became too severe the men could be laid off without pay and they would have remained very insecure in their employment.

'I should recommend that labourers themselves have to provide certain tools. I should also recommend that the workmen be paid weekly on account ten or fifteen per cent of what is due to them, merely to prevent mistakes; then settle

the whole at the end of each month. Pay the contractor off entirely and let them start afresh at the commencement of the month following. It is, however, desirable to keep one running week, alias, one week in hand.'

In the 1830s the new reservoir project brought much needed labour for the people of Entwistle over four years and at least one third of the workforce came from the township.

A random example from the work payments book of 1836 is as follows:

May   *John Yates, Whitehead Cote, 21¼ days work @ 3 shillings per day paid £3 3s 9d less sub, paid £1 10s 0d. Balance £1 13s 9d for earth moving.*
         Alice Brigg, Lower House, (carter), 7 days work @ 8/6 per day = £2 19s 6d.

July   *George Briggs, Lower House (puddler), 5 days work @ 2s per day = 10s.*
         John Brigg, Lower House (forman), 1 week wage = £1 0s 0d.

Aug   *Thomas Brigg, New Hall Farms (puddler), 4¾ days @ 2s 10d per day = 13s. 5½ d.*

Sept   *John Brigg, (overlooker),£4 9s 6d less sub 9/6 Balance £4 0s 0d.*
         John Waddica, Crow Trees (carpenter),6¾ days @ 3/6 per day Balance £1 3s 7½d.

The pay book lists some men working 15 to 30 days without a break; they were obviously fit young fellows doing this back breaking work. Carters were expected to help load and to unload their carts. The cost of the works finally amounted to £16,700 plus £3,000 legal expenses.

8.2   BOLTON IMPROVEMENT ACT 1865

Not enough of the downstream industries made payment towards the cost of building the reservoir and the initial debt could not be repaid. Consequently under the Bolton Improvement Act 1864 the corporation acquired the reservoir *'together with all the estates, land, rights, privileges, easements, arrears of rates and other property of the Commissioners'*. The corporation not only paid the mortgage debt of the Commissioners of £26,997 11s 3d but also the outstanding interest of £7,553 9s 0d.

In the preamble to the Act, the corporation were also empowered '*to acquire a reservoir called the Turton and Entwistle Reservoir and to construct additional waterworks and* (amongst other things) *a reservoir to be called the Wayoh Reservoir and are required to supply, by means of pipes, clean water to the occupiers of certain falls in the stream between the Wayoh Reservoir and the junction of Bradshaw Brook with Tonge.*'

The construction of the Wayoh Reservoir took 10 years (1866-1876). Only then did the waters of the Entwistle Reservoir become available to Bolton Corporation for drinking water. The corporation constructed a tunnel between Entwistle Reservoir and Dimple. It was 3,070 yards long, five feet in diameter, and was driven under Turton Heights between the valleys of the Bradshaw and Eagley Brooks so as to bring clean water to a convenient place where it could enter the town's supply.

In the Act the compensation water delivered into Bradshaw Brook from the new Wayoh Reservoir was to exceed 3,827,140 gallons per day. It had to be more than the 3,700,000 gallons per day of drinking water made available to Bolton from Entwistle Reservoir.

The original Entwistle dam was constructed as an earthfill embankment with a central puddle clay core in 1836 and runs across Bradshaw Brook. It was 360ft long and 108ft high, the highest in Britain when built. The height of the dam was raised in 1990.

At the northeastern end of the dam there is a masonry spillway which allows water to discharge down a stone cascade into Bradshaw Brook, which then feeds directly into the Wayoh Reservoir. In 1838 the spillway entrance was 24 metres wide but was reduced in 1990 to 3 metres to improve the capacity of the reservoir. In 2006 work was again carried out on the spillway channel to reduce the likelihood of blockage from fallen trees and other debris during heavy storms. The drystone wall across the top of the dam alongside the road has been rebuilt using a reinforced concrete core and clad in a natural stone to improve wave protection and increase the flood capacity of the dam. This work ensures that the reservoir remains safe during a 'Probable Maximum Flood'; a 1 in 10,000 years storm!

8.3   OULDEN FOLD

Situated on the southern slopes of lower Cadshaw Valley, Oulden Fold was probably the largest hamlet in Entwistle until it was lost under the reservoir. It included a cluster of ancient cottages together with a farmhouse, and dotted around this beautiful site were other fine properties including 'Ould Ralphs' 'Barlows', 'Ould Livings' 'Simms' and 'Lower House' or 'Entwistle New Hall'.

At the time of the Tyldesley sale of 1657, Oulden Fold was in the possession of Hugh Entwistle, father of John, a trustee and purchaser of part of the Tyldesley Estate. Its importance can be appreciated from the annual township property tax levied at two shillings on Oulden Fold and on other properties including: Ould Ralphs 7¾d, Barlows 11d, Ould Livings 18d, Entwistle Hall (Lower House) 4 shillings.

The last residents of the place were the Mayor family. Peter Mayor stayed in his house and firmly declined to leave this lovely place, but when the valley was finally flooded he had to be rescued from the roof of his home at the last moment and long after his family and neighbours had departed. Another displaced former resident was William Entwistle, alias 'Mussel Billy', a well known hawker of cockles and mussels.

Entwistle Reservoir from the east in 1948.

Entwistle Reservoir from the west in 2009.

Entwistle Reservoir and dam.

Water tower on the reservoir dam.

A commemorative iron casting
on the reservoir dam.

Harry Jolly, water
bailiff at Entwistle.

85

Harry Jolly examining the water pipe in the tunnel
between Entwistle and Delph Reservoirs.

Flow measuring device at Entwistle Reservoir, c1868.

CHAPTER IX   THE RAILWAY

9.1   PROMOTING THE LINE

With the opening of the outstandingly successful railway from Bolton to Leigh, in 1829, followed by the line from Bolton to Manchester in 1838, the mill owners of Blackburn, Darwen and Bolton at last decided to invest in a new rail link from Blackburn through to Bolton with the aim of getting goods carried more cheaply than by the alternative wagon and horse transport, which at that time cost an average of 10d per mile per ton between Blackburn and Manchester where all the raw cotton and finished goods were bought or sold.

Completion of the Bolton to Manchester railway impelled local businessmen into action and a meeting was arranged at the Greenway Arms Inn in Darwen in 1844. The assembly was chaired by Mr John Fowden Hindle Esq., of Woodfold Park, Blackburn, High Sheriff of Lancaster and addressed by Mr John Watson, a prominent engineer who had previously surveyed a route between Blackburn, Darwen, Sough, Entwistle and Edgworth to Bolton for a two line track. His estimate was £213,600 and it was agreed to fix the capital needed at £300,000; not surprisingly as some of the proposed land for the track had not yet been purchased.

Shares priced at £25 each went on sale to the public. The major holders were Mr William Henry Hornby Esq; Mr John Fowden Hindle Esq, Blackburn; Eccles Shorrocks, Cotton Merchant, Darwen; Charles Potter, Wallpaper Manufacturer, Darwen; James Kay, Cotton Spinner, Turton; Thomas Eccles, Darwen; John Brandwood of Darwen and Henry Ashworth & Bros. of Eagley Mills, Bolton.

The Blackburn, Darwen and Bolton Railway received its Charter of Incorporation from Parliament on the 30th June 1845. Mr Charles Blacker Vignoles was appointed the consulting engineer with Mr Terry as his assistant. In September 1845 the construction contract was let to a Mr John Evans Sen., of Oldham. September 27th saw Mr Henry Hornby Esq. cut the first turf in the centre of Darwen and so began the first part of the line between Darwen and Whittlestone Head.

9.2   PRIVILEGES AND RIGHTS OF WAY

So keen were the railway agents to persuade landowners to sell, that at times they would agree to some odd condition. For example, when selling 6 acres of his land for Walton sidings Mr Thomas Whitehead, owner of Whitehead Cote Farm, insisted that the terms of sale guaranteed the occupier of the farm right of passage along the permanent way for *'all time'* when using Entwistle Station, a distance of 1,200 yards, instead of having to go by the road, a distance of 3 miles. This right was exercised without restriction, certainly from 1943 to 1973, by Mr Jack Lewis, owner of Whitehead Cote Farm, and from 1973 to 2000 by the author.

A 21 acre field, purchased for £175 from Mr William Whitehead at Overhouses in 1847, was used for a deep cutting, commencing where a road bridge crossed the track beyond Turton station, and continuing northward for three hundred yards to the Entwistle viaduct. A provision under the terms of sale gave the occupier of Overhouses the right of passage along the permanent way when using Turton Station, with an access gate set in the garden for that purpose, instead of having to go much further round by the road.

9.3   SOUGH TUNNEL

The first route proposed by Vignoles was for a conventional line from Bolton up to the hamlet of Whittlestone Head, then up an incline to Pinnacle Nook, Hoddlesden by means of winch operated wire (as on the Bolton to Leigh line) then the train could run down a similar incline to Darwen.

An alternative to the incline was the tunnel under Cranberry Moss from Whittlestone Head to Sough Village, a distance of some 2015 yards. Cranberry Moss was a badly drained waste land rising up to over 1000 feet above sea level and then, as now, riddled with old colliery workings.

The first problem Mr Evans, the Contractor encountered was the recruitment of specialist tunnellers who had to be enticed away from coal mines in Yorkshire, Wigan and Wales with the promise of high wages. The unskilled part of the work force was mainly of Irish descent and eventually some 2,000 men were working on the tunnel project. The plan was to sink 13 shafts in line across the Moss with depths varying from 40ft to 260ft deep then drive headings between them to make a continuous tunnel.

With candles, hand drills and gunpowder, for over two years, the miners cut the tunnel through sandstone, shale, clay, and occasional coal seams at a gradient of 1 in 74 until it was over one mile in length and lined with stone and brick.. The height of the tunnel varied between 22ft. and 24ft. and the width was 24ft.

Even now on a dry summer's day the tunnel is damp and has a foul earthy smell. The walls run with water and the cold is penetrating. The only relief the miners would have had was from large quantities of raw whiskey said to have been distilled from illicit stills concealed in the various mine workings.

A most macabre incident is recorded during the construction. Two Turton men, a father and son, were employed to fill shaft No 5 from a wooden stage spread across the 10ft diameter surface opening. An overnight storm had washed out much of the loose earth from under the platform where it rested on the edge of the shaft. When both men stepped on to the delicately poised planking, it tilted sharply downwards plunging them to their deaths 100ft below. An avalanche of stony rubble cascading down the partly filled cavity effectively entombed them. Attempts to retrieve their bodies, and that of a labourer who fell into shaft No 9, were eventually abandoned and some weeks later the openings were completely closed.

Shaft No 6, rising midway along the tunnel, was the deepest of them all and it claimed twelve years old Billy Godbhere as a victim. His job was to run to the smithy with picks that the men had sent up for re-sharpening. When whiling away the hours waiting and watching the hopper as it came up the shaft laden with spoil for tipping, he gave the hopper a playful swing, it rebounded and knocked the hapless child over the brink of the 260ft shaft.

The shafts were filled when construction of the tunnel ended, but in 1903 the Lancashire and Yorkshire Railway, who then owned the line, reopened shafts No 4 and No 9 (158ft and 210ft deep respectively) to improve the ventilation. This was particularly desirable in days when steam locomotives were exclusively used to haul slow moving goods trains .

As one would expect with over 2000 men, plus women and children, engaged in building the line through Whittlestone Head, there were many social problems, in this quiet back-water. The construction workers and their families were camped in the fields around the hamlet for over two years. Law and order was practically non-existent and living on this bleak hillside in shelters open to the elements made for a hard life.

Labouring six days a week for a gold sovereign, navvies working in shifts, sometimes moved as much as 22 cubic yards of earth per shift. Women and children often worked alongside their men folk without pay. Men sometimes started work at 4 am so as to finish their quota on time. Gambling and fighting seemed to be their main pastimes, clog fighting almost naked for a five pound wager was common practice. One Irishman's favourite trick was to bet anyone he could hang by a rope tied round his neck from a ceiling beam, the price of this wager was five pounds. He had performed the trick many times, but sadly in 1847 at Whittlestone Head Tavern, he lost his bet.

Makeshift shelters for railway navvies. Such structures were in use during construction at Whittlestone Head, 1845-1848.

Tunnelling in the 1840s using blackpowder and hand drills.

C B Vignoles, Engineer.

'MAZEPPA' an early LYR engine.

The local populace took a dim view of all this unlawful behaviour and requested extra police for the area, but Mr John Evans Jnr, the contract foreman, refused the request.

Ale could be had at any time at Greenhalgh's Inn, Whittlestone Head, that is until the Revenue Inspector closed it down for selling illegal spirits. The licence was then transferred to the Railway Tavern a small farm just a few yards away. Drunken brawls were an all too common occurrence.

By far the most irksome problem the railway had to deal with was the fouling of Whittlestone Head Brook that normally supplied crystal clear water to Know Mill, owned by Messrs Roxburgh and Ashworth. After months of lost production and much litigation, the railway company settled a claim for £5000.

9.4 BRADSHAW BROOK VIADUCT

One striking feature of the railway line is the fine viaduct built to cross the deep, wooded ravine through which Bradshaw Brook snakes its way to Bolton. Finding and transporting the right type of stone for this rather dainty looking nine span structure, which stands 100 feet high from the river bed, proved quite a problem for the resident procurement officer, Mr Evans. It was eventually built of hammer dressed stone, each block weighs 3 tons and the foundation stones were of strong gritstone.

9.5 RAIL SERVICES

The inaugural run to Bolton took place on Monday 12th June 1848 at 7.05 a.m. A regular service train made up of eight carriages packed to capacity left Blackburn drawn by a Hawthorn 0-6-0 engine and the journey to Bolton was completed in thirty eight minutes.

The company's timetable listed six trains on weekdays to Bolton and Salford (for Manchester) and the same in the reverse direction. There were three trains each way on Sundays. Initially passengers were conveyed in three classes of carriage, as under the Railways Act of 1844, third class passengers had to be conveyed and accommodated in closed compartments with seats at a charge not exceeding one penny per mile. All railway companies were legally bound to provide these facilities on at least one train per day known as a 'Parliamentary'. In this way rail travel became available to all but the poorest section of society. The effect the coming of the railway had on Entwistle was enormous.

In the early years of the line, trains stopped near to Walton Sidings but no buildings seem to have been provided, other than a signal box; nothing else is shown on the map. By 1884 Entwistle had up and down lines and a loop. On a contemporary plan there is a dotted line indicating a projected new road from the bridge over the line down to an area which was to become the goods yard and this same development is shown on the plan submitted by the Inspector of Railways to the Board of Trade, on 18th February 1876. It stated, '*I have inspected the* new *connections at Entwistle between Bolton and Blackburn. The proposed arrangements are satisfactory with the following exceptions. The necessity for a siding on the down line because of the sharp incline*'. This was in case of a train brake failure, a runaway train could be directed off the line, otherwise it would roll with increasing momentum down to Bolton. He also advised that the up and down starting signals should be moved.

On the Inspector's plan there are no station buildings other than a '*Brick Signal Cabin*' of 18x11ft. This must have been the original signal box, including as '*Apparatus*', '*6 point levers, 8 signal levers, 4 spare levers*'. Walton sidings are not shown on either the 1876 or 1884 plans.

By 1892 a new station building was in place complete with sidings. The Station Master, then Mr Richard Caldwell, was ably supported by ten staff. Mr Caldwell lived at the station master's house in the new Railway Terrace just behind Bridge House, the home of Mr William Horrocks, farmer and beer seller. This house was later named The Station Hotel, now the Strawbury Duck. In 1884 the goods yard and warehouse buildings were completed. The justification for such development seems to have been the increased production at Know Mill, which in the 1890s had a workforce of over 200 people and was less than 200 yards from the station.

In 1904, Entwistle Station was enlarged to accommodate four lines instead of two, with more sidings and many new buildings. The Railway Inspector wrote: '*In 1904 Entwistle Station had been remodelled and was now an island platform between the up and down slow lines, approached by a staircase from a new bridge.*' It was now 596 feet long, three feet above rail level and of sufficient width, with good accommodation for both sexes. There were now four lines running through the station, two slow and two fast lines. A new signal box, containing 43 working levers, 9 spare levers and 8 spaces, had been built on a gantry 10 feet high spanning the fast lines. A branch line going north went to Walton Sidings where it served the stone quarry at Round Barn. There was also an overhead ropeway link to Know Mill. The land for this expansion had come from G.W.Heywood of New Hall House for a consideration of £565-11s.

LYR train on Entwistle viaduct with Wayoh reservoir in the background.

Entwistle Station and goods yard in LYR days.

'Railway Terrace' at Entwistle Station: built by the LYR c1904 for railwaymen. The stationmaster's house is at the left end of the terrace.

Entwistle Station, signal box and disused goods yard in 1965. (Photograph supplied by John Wolfenden.)

Banking engine leaving its train at Walton Summit, 1968 (from 'Steam World').

Two 'Black Fives' on a steeply graded section of the near Walton Siding (from Steam World).

Southbound goods trains leaving Sough Tunnel.

A driver on the Bolton-Blackburn line.

Derelict signalbox at Walton Sidings, 1973.

Ben Pilling, signalman at Entwistle Station.

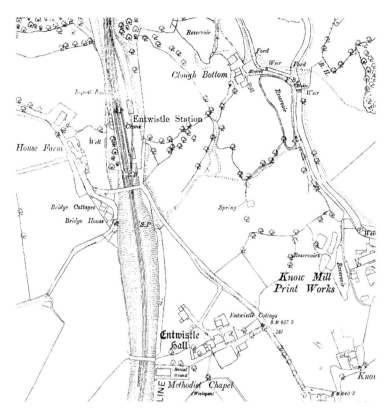

25 inch OS map of 1891 showing Entwistle Station before it was enlarged.

9.7   CLOSURE THREAT

The railway at Entwistle continued to provide a useful public service for well over a century. However a disaster almost happened in 1962 when Dr Beeching, then Minister of Transport, proposed the closure of many branch lines and stations including Entwistle. A rearguard action, organised by the residents and ably assisted by Mrs Blair then of New Hall, saved the day. A much reduced train service resulted, which in turn had repercussions for the prosperity of the Station Hotel. In 1960 Thwaites brewery put the pub on the market but again the residents fought the closure until a Mr Ducksbury bought and transformed it into a very popular venue. Although the pub's future was secured, the railway station had a more precarious life and in 1994 closure was again proposed. Residents had yet another fight on their hands but were successful again in saving the station and the public service it continues to provide.

'*Christine Alken, Irene Jones and Joyce Nelson arrange trips from their remote homes in Entwistle around the railway Timetable.*'

'*Milly and Clive Walsh fear they may have to leave the remote splendour of their Cote Farm if the train service is cut.*'

'*Entwistle villagers gather for the oncoming train. They want more trains rather than the slashed service that BR plans to enforce.*'

'*Entwistle born Alf Mitton and his wife Barbara rely heavily on the train service for travel as diverse as shopping and going to the dentist.*'

Photographs with captions from a Bolton Evening News article of 1992 in support of the campaign to save Entwistle Station. The report mentions '*the wild and beautiful countryside around Entwistle, served by a single line train service and a narrow road*'.

CHAPTER X   EXTRACTIVE INDUSTRIES

10.1   COAL AND FIRECLAY

Cranberry Moss

The first record of coal mining in Entwistle seems to be in the sale of the Tyldesley Estate in 1670 when, as mentioned earlier, Edward Tyldesley retained one half of the rights to mine coal on the 'commons' in Entwistle, which meant Cranberry and Aushaw Mosses. The other half went to Norbury and Lowe who, acting as agents for certain of the tenants, would have sold them on.

One of those with an interest in coal mining was James Kay of Edgefold Farm who c1784 recorded that he and others had had gone to great deal of trouble, and expense over a coal mine. There is no information about the location of the mine, but it seems likely that Kay's interest derived from a right to mine on the commons land mentioned in the Tyldesley sales.

Otherwise there is evidence of mining in Entwistle on Yates' map of 1786. Here a single shaft on Cranberry Moss is marked *'coal pit'*, the only one so recorded in the whole parish of Bolton-le-Moors, although there were many other collieries in existence at that time, but for some reason Yates chose to show this one. The colliery was located on Cranberry Moss and linked by a track to the Roman Road across the township boundary near to *'Stoops'* (Drummer Stoops). At that time the Roman Road probably offered a better route for delivering coal than the alternative old highway over Bull Hill.

However the better road was not long in coming in the form of the Bolton to Blackburn Turnpike. When this was first promoted, in 1798, a plan was made of preferred routes which showed an alternative line for the road that, although never built, was intended to run from the new Cadshaw Bridge, over *'Entwistle Moss'* (Cranberry Moss) and then through Sough into Darwen, passing the *'Entwistle Coal Mine'* on the Moss, in much the same position as the coal mine on Yates' Plan. Shallow collieries in Lancashire used multiple shafts at that time and it is unlikely that the colliery on Cranberry Moss consisted of the single shaft shown. What is shown was probably the main site of the colliery.

Mining in common land remained under the control of the Lord of the Manor, unless the estate, or at least the mining rights, had been sold off, in which case access to the coal and royalties were a matter for negotiation between the interested parties. Some examples of these transactions at Entwistle survive. The first was an indenture of 1821 when Samuel Woodcock of Holcombe and

William Scoles of Leigh bought a share of coal and cannel in Entwistle from William Wood (Little Bolton), Roger Ward (Minister of Kidderminster) and Mary and Elizabeth Pilkington (Blackburn). In following year (1822) there was another indenture concerning Samuel and James Woodcock who bought a share in the coal under *'Entwistle Mosses'* from Richard and James Kay (yeomen) and John Ainsworth (cotton manufacturer), both of Turton, while in 1829 Thomas Kay, a bankrupt, sold his share of the *'mine of cannel and coal and other minerals under the common wastes in Entwistle'*. Thomas Kay lived at Edge foot and was trying to sell his interest in the minerals, to offset his debts.

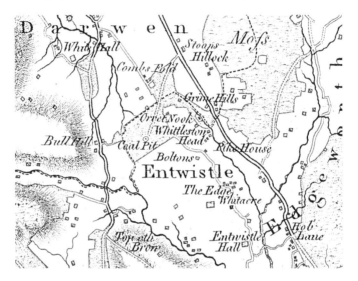

Yates' map of 1785 showing a coal pit in Entwistle.

In a further indenture of 1834 *'Messrs Hilton'* and William Eccles bought shares from the Woodcocks for coal under Entwistle and Lower Aushaw mosses. The Woodcocks worked coal under Entwistle Moss until 1834. Hiltons, who then took over, were paper makers in Darwen. They had extensive operations and are probably responsible for most of the workings recorded on the six inch OS map surveyed in 1844-47.

There is a reference to Hiltons' operations in the obituary of William Taylor, former managing director at Turton Moor Colliery, who died in 1916. Mention is made of his father Ellis Taylor, one time mine manager for Hiltons at Dogshaw (Duckshaw) Colliery on Darwen Moor and who once *'bored pits for Hiltons on Cranberry Moss'*. Hiltons again appear in the statistical survey of power sources carried out in 1837 where the firm of H & E Hilton is recorded as having one steam engine of 6 horse power at their colliery in Entwistle.

Although the OS map shows a large number of coal pits on Cranberry Moss, that probably belonged to Hiltons, none of these seemed to be operating when the survey was made. Hiltons suffered a financial failure about this time, a situation which might well have resulted in the temporary cessation of mining and ultimate need to sell their interests in the coal.

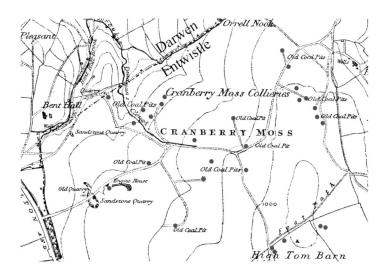

Cranberry Moss Collieries: 1844-47.

After Hiltons had given up their mining activities, Eccles Shorrock became involved and was recorded by the Inspector of Mines as having a colliery at *'Entwistle Moss.'* His was the only colliery in Entwistle in 1855, but he appears again in the Inspector's lists in 1861 and in each succeeding year until 1865.

By 1860 the common land at Entwistle had become the subject of an Enclosure scheme that involved, among other things, the making of a special map of the area. This shows two operating collieries on Cranberry Moss, each with its own engine house, on separate plots that were awarded to Walker Hulton of Ainsworth and to John Heywood respectively. The text of the enclosure award makes no mention of either colliery both of which seem to have been operated by Eccles Shorrock at that time.

Although the multiple shafts used by Hiltons contrast with the two shafts used in 1860, the difference results from changes in working practice that occurred about this time. Ventilation principles were becoming better understood allowing air to be circulated throughout the workings from far fewer entrances.

Also underground haulage improved so that a single properly equipped shaft was becoming the preferred way of bringing the coal to the surface, whereas previously shafts had been sunk to keep up with the advancing workings.

At Cranberry Moss, two seams, Upper Mountain Mine and Lower Mountain Mine are present, they are inclined towards the south west and the coalfield is bounded on the west side by a large fault running close to the A666 and on the east by a fault running parallel to the railway near Sough Tunnel. Between the two several more or less parallel faults also break up the strata.

The Lower Mountain Mine was a good coking coal as is evidenced by three old 'beehive' coke ovens on Cranberry Moss, clearly visible from the main road. Although a little thicker and easier to access, the upper seam apparently contained some stony material and for this reason was less sought after.

From 1865 to 1870 James Barlow is on the record for coal mining, first at 'Whittlestone Head' then at 'Cranberry Moss'. There is no evidence as to exactly where his mines were located or even if they were completely separate operations. However James Barlow, one of the beneficiaries from the Enclosure, had acquired a parcel of coal-bearing land near Sough Tunnel and this was probably the site of his activities.

The long final phase of extraction at Cranberry Moss is focused on the activities of Ralph Entwistle Ltd, a Darwen fireclay manufacturer. His main interest was in working the Lower Mountain Mine and the valuable fireclay seam with which it is associated. Fireclay producers often did not sell coal but used it to fire the kilns to make the fireclay articles which were mainly sewage pipes.

Ralph Entwistle first appears in the list of mines operating on Cranberry Moss in 1871 and then each year in the same way until 1885 when the firm is also listed as mining at 'Cranberry Lane, Darwen'. Operations after 1885 are then confined to Darwen until 1894 when they appear again in both places.

What appears to have happened is that Ralph Entwistle had a fireclay works on Cranberry Moss and established a mine there that ran from 1871 until 1885. In that year (1885) he erected the 'Darwen Fireclay Works', and sunk a new shaft alongside, just over the township boundary in Cranberry Lane, Darwen. About 1894 the company extended a long tunnel from the then current workings in Darwen, across the township and parish boundary, into the old workings on Cranberry Moss. Coal and fireclay could then be hauled underground to the winding shaft alongside the works. This arrangement operated until 1915 when the colliery was abandoned after the company had become insolvent.

Another fireclay producer, known as Bull Hill Fire Clay Works is shown on the 25 inch OS map of 1891. It consisted of 3 kilns and associated buildings located to the north of Tom Barn, but otherwise nothing much is known about it.

New House

The Bolton Chronicle in 1831 carried the following notice of a sale:-

'At Bridge Inn Bolton on 27 July 1831'.
'New House Estate, formerly part of Entwistle Hall Estate in Bolton, now divided into two farms: one of 12 acres (Cheshire) tenanted by James Mather under a lease that expires in Spring 1837: the other of 15 acres (Cheshire) occupied by Isaac Mather: together with mines of coal, cannel and ironstone within the estate and the steam engine of 16 hp, engine house, pumps, pit and shafts etc now on the premises for working the mines. The Engine Pit is sunk 5½ yds below the higher bed of coal and the engine is of sufficient power to work the two lower mines of coal as well as the ironstone'.

Although there is no information in the sale notice about the location of this operation, the six inch OS map, surveyed 1844-47, records the single shaft of an *'old coal pit'* near to New Hall farm and the then new Entwistle railway station. The mine is not located in the Coal Measures but in the Millstone Grit where a few thin coal seams are occasionally found together, in this particular location, with some ironstones.

The colliery was located on an obviously poor mineral reserve. Consequently it does not seem to have lasted long, or ever amounted to much, it is even doubtful whether the owner managed to sell it at the auction.

Aushaw Moss

J.J Place's colliery at Hoddlesden sank a shaft in Edgworth called No 12 in the 1930s and by the 1950s some of these workings, in both the Lower and Upper Mountain Mines, extended into a small part of Entwistle on the west side of Orrell Moss but there was never any shaft or other access in Entwistle.

Otherwise there are also a few shafts into shallow workings on Aushaw Moss. These comprise a limited extension of the operations of the former Broadhead Colliery which was located near Naze End, just over the township boundary in Edgworth. The workings were not recorded by the Inspector of Mines, and must have been completed before 1853, although they seem to have been in operation when the first OS map was surveyed in1844-7.

Remains of early nineteenth century 'beehive' coke ovens on Cranberry Moss.

Round Barn Quarry.

10.2   STONE

It is possible that the first quarrying at Round Barn was done by the Brandwoods in a small way during the late 17th century. However the first record of quarrying on a map is seen on the six inch OS of 1847 and even then the worked area is quite small; less than a quarter of that of the quarry at Edgworth (adjacent to Wayoh Reservoir). Early workings would probably be sufficient only for local needs, until the railway arrived. Then large amounts of stone would be needed for construction and the finished railway might enable quarry products to be distributed over a large area.

Baines' Directory in 1824 lists Ralph Knowles as a stone merchant and master builder at Entwistle and the Knowles family certainly owned Round Barn Quarry when Aushaw Moss was Enclosed in 1859. *'Widow Entwistle and Son'* are also listed as stone merchants but there is no indication as to which quarry, if any, was owned.

With the railway under construction a rope-worked rail incline from Round Barn Quarry down to Walton Sidings enabled loaded wagons to be sent from the quarry directly to the railway.

From 1848-1885 stone seems to have been quarried in a modest way at Round Barn with various people renting the quarry on a short lease which was a common practice at that time. By 1891 the quarry had been abandoned and the rail incline dismantled.

In 1896 the quarry was reopened by Rudman and Phillipson Ltd sometimes trading as *'The Railway and Walton Quarry and Brick Co Ltd'* and the rail incline was restored. The main interest of the company seems to have been the underground mining of flagstone from levels at the base of the old quarry face. The workings had become quite extensive by the time the quarry finally closed. The rough flagstones needed careful dressing to get them to the right shape and thickness for pavement slabs and hence the quarry would have employed a large labour force.

The quarry extracted a formation known as the Haslingden Flags which was also worked on a very large scale in Rossendale. At one time Haslingden Flags provided the major source of paving flags for Lancashire and were quite important nationally. The other products from Round Barn Quarry consisted of sawn doorsteps, window heads, window sills, curbs and edging stone, the most expensive products being polished stone slabs used at Know Mill and in the textile printing industry generally. Unfortunately for the natural flagstone producers, concrete paving stones, began to appear in the 1920. They could be made near to where they were needed, had more precise dimensions and above all were cheaper than flags. This led to the closure of most of the flagstone quarries and the demise of what had once been an important Lancashire industry.

Like so many others, Round Barn Quarry finally closed in the mid 1920s and has remained idle ever since, but in its prime it produced flagstones on a considerable scale. An old Entwistle resident, Mr Pat Hatzar, speaking to the author in the 1970s said he could remember, as a youth in the 1920s, forty empty railway wagons being brought to Walton Sidings early in the morning and by late evening the full wagons being shunted down the line to Entwistle station to join the main line for delivery to Bolton, and other local towns.

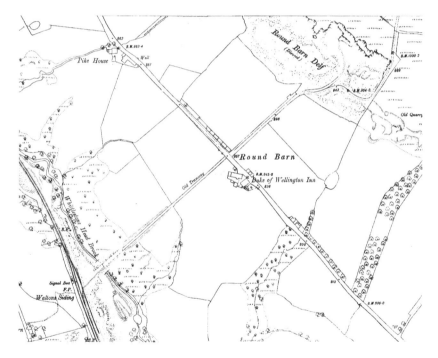

25 inch OS map of 1891, Round Barn Quarry was disused at this time and the *'old tramway'* incline connecting it with Walton Sidings had been lifted.

An entrance to the underground flagstone workings at Round Barn Quarry.

Old tramway incline at Round Barn Quarry.

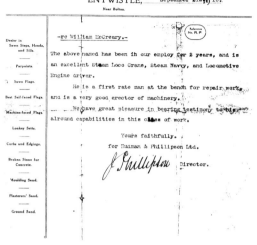

Dealer in
Sawn Steps, Heads,
and Sills.

Parpoints.

Sawn Flags.

Best Self-faced Flags.

Machine-faced Flags.

Lonkey Setts.

Curbs and Edgings.

Broken Stone for
Concrete.

Moulding Sand.

Plasterers' Sand.

Ground Sand.

—re William McCreary.—

Reference
No. R.P.

The above named has been in our employ for 2 years, and is an excellent Steam Loco Crane, Steam Navvy, and Locomotive Engine driver.

He is a first rate man at the bench for repair work, and is a very good erector of machinery.

We have great pleasure in bearing testimony to his allround capabilities in this class of work.

Yours faithfully,

for Rudman & Phillipson Ltd.

J. Phillipson Director.

Reference issued by Round Barn Quarry in 1915 for William McCreary.

10.3   BRICK

On the 31st July 1896 the Turton Urban District Council received the following application: ' *Sirs, we The Railway and Walton Quarry and Brick Co Ltd of 68 Port Street, Manchester, a Company formed in 1896 to mine stone at Round Barn Quarry also propose to build a Brickworks, and rail tracks worked by a wire rope to a new brickworks at new Walton sidings' –'The Walton Brick Co.'* Thus the company gave notice of their intention to erect a new brickworks at Walton Sidings alongside the railway and to re-lay the rails on the incline past the brickworks and up to Round Barn Quarry.

By 1903, as the newly enlarged Entwistle Station neared completion, another brick making venture was started by the same company less than three hundred yards away and known as the Blackhill Brick and Terracotta Co Ltd.

A document dated 31st December 1903 reads:
'The trustee under the will of the late Mr William Heywood Esq., of New Hall, to the Blackhill Brick and Terracotta Company Ltd, in such consideration of the rent...the trustee hereby grant the lessees full liberty and licence to and for

constructing, laying and maintaining, a single line of tramway, of two feet gauge on part of the occupation road and pathway through the existing subway....and there under the railway bridge erected in the field numbered 58, the "Calf Meadow".

Thus Rudman and Phillipsons, in addition to Round Barn Stone Quarry, also established Blackhill Brickworks and Walton Brickworks. At Blackhill Brickworks they installed nine kilns, two tramways, four clay settlement tanks, a stone crushing house and two mixing houses. A substantial stone quarry was also opened in Bank Wood, and a huge shale pit was dug at Whitehead's Farm.

The tramway connection to the station goods yard made it practical to sell Blackhill products over a wide area. The range of brick and terracotta ware produced at the works was truly amazing. Red, yellow and orange brickwork came in every conceivable shape and size, made from a mixture of crushed stone, various clays and coloured sands in *'secret mixes'* from which 'Blackhill Plastic Brick' was made.

Many local buildings were constructed with this new brick: St James' Church at Hob Lane; Red Brick Row in Edgworth; Railway Terrace on Overshores Road, Entwistle and two bungalows, East and West dated 1911, standing on Rose Tree Lane, Entwistle. East bungalow was the company's office until the brickworks closed in 1930 and West bungalow was the manager's house.

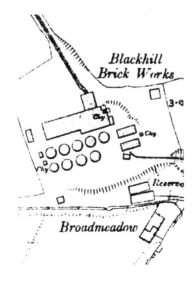

Plan of the Blackhill Brickworks c1910.

111

East Bungalow: one of the two bungalows on Rose Tree Lane built by the
Blackhill Brick Company

Terracotta signs on adjacent bungalows at the brickworks of the Blackhill Brick
Company. West Bungalow was the manager's house and East Bungalow the
company office.

The tunnel under the railway that accommodated the tramway
from Blackhill Brickworks to Entwistle Station.

A 'Blackhill Plastic' brick

10.4   PEAT

Another small industry in Entwistle that had a brief life was started on Lower Aushaw Moor by a Mr Stanley Johnson of Round Barn Farm. He recovered peat from the Moss and sold it mainly for agricultural purposes.

In 1941/42 the government spent time and money lowering and draining part of the peat covered moor in a plan to build an airfield for short take-off aircraft, which never came to fruition.

By 1947 Mr Johnson's business continued on a small scale. Loose loads of peat were taken to Hindley Green by one Joseph Robinson, a haulier of Darwen, for processing and ultimate use in poultry farming. After Mr Johnson retired Mr Fred Loads set up the 'Eclipse Peat Company' in a converted Nissen hut, to work peat on the lower part of the moor. This time the product was sold as 'peat moss' for use in horticulture in John Innes compost grow bags and in peat bales.

The high part of the moor in the 1950s came into the ownership of Fisons Fertilizers who worked it for 'sedge peat' which was in great demand for use in the purification of coal gas. For over 10 years Olafe Frazer and his brothers worked the moor and transported countless loads of 'sedge peat' to various gas works in Lancashire and Yorkshire until North Sea gas came on-stream in 1969 after which their contract ceased.

The Frazer Brothers then took over the old Eclipse Peat works to continue in the business but with little success.

In the late 1970s a planning application was made for permission to extract peat to a depth in excess of six feet, which was refused on ground that it might result in contamination of the water draining into Wayoh Reservoir, then owned by North West Water. The peat works finally closed in the 1980s and there has been no extraction since.

CHAPTER X1   ENCLOSURES

11.1   ENTWISTLE FREEHOLDERS

Entwistle freeholders were involved in two enclosures. The first was actually in Edgworth but such was the association between the two townships that several Entwistle residents benefited by being awarded land. The details are fully described in an earlier publication of the Society (No 7).

By the middle of the nineteenth century all the common land in the Parish of Bolton le Moors had been enclosed except for two poorly drained upland areas in Entwistle which, until then, had perhaps been of too little value to be worth the effort. The land comprised two separate mosses known as Cranberry Moss and Aushaw Moss, which in 1859 finally became the subject of an enclosure procedure. These were fairly extensive areas but both consisted of somewhat bleak, inhospitable tracts, which to a large extent have retained their character to the present day.

11.2   ENCLOSURE OF EDGWORTH MOOR

In 1672 Freeholders of Edgworth and Entwistle agreed, after many years of bickering, to place the division of the ancient common lands called Edgworth Moor in the hands of arbitrators. The arbitrators were Henry Knowles, yeoman, of Edgworth and Francis Norbury, yeoman, of Entwistle.

They ordered that '*the several and respective freeholders of Entwistle and their heirs shall have four score acres of Edgworth Moors enclosed by stone wall or ditch.*' It included an order '*to keep the walls etc in good repair, also no stopping up of waterways.*' It also ordered that '*the freeholders and their heirs shall have two ways within Edgworth aforesaid, betwixt the hamlet of Entwistle and the said common called Edgworth moor. The one way by and through the lane called Hob Lane and the other by and through the common highway leading betwixt Weoh Bridge and the said Hob Lane, and at the Hob Lane gate, the said two ways to meet, and from thence but one way to and from the said Entwistle part of the common by the new house there lately built by George Longworth, or in some convenient place betwixt said new house and the said cross standing on Edgworth Low, to be appointed and set out by the freeholders of Edgworth aforesaid, their heirs or assigns, and that there shall be one gate and no more for passage into the said Entwistle part of the common.*'
They further ordered '*the freeholders of Edgworth to have all the rest and the residue of the great common called Edgworth moor.*'

Sealed, signed and delivered in the presence of Richard Orrell and Jeremiah Ainsworth

| *Entwistle freeholders:* | *John Entwistle, James Brandwood, William Horrocks, David Whitehead, Peter Kay, Ralph Entwistle* |
| *Edgworth Freeholders:* | *Thomas Thomason, Robert Isherwood, Robert Isherwood* |

(Peter Kay, Ralph Entwistle and Robert Isherwood made their mark.)

11.3   CRANBERRY MOSS AND AUSHAW MOSS AWARD

In 1859 Cranberry and Aushaw Mosses became the subject of an enclosure procedure. Enclosure at that time required an Act of Parliament, usually initiated when a group of freeholders in the township got together to promote the Act and then arrange for the enclosed land to be divided, usually amongst themselves and thus pass into private ownership. The enclosure process might be complicated by people who had taken over some part of the land without authority (encroachments) and might also affect other inhabitants who were not freeholders but had long used the common for grazing. There seems to have been little difficulty getting the Act through and the enclosure was completed by January 1860. The procedure involved appointing a commissioner who surveyed the lands, divided them up among the various interested parties in proportion to their holdings in the township, arranged for any access or occupation roads to be built, specified where fences were to be placed and reported accordingly.

The enclosure of Cranberry Moss and Aushaw Moss can be summarized in the following tables detailing the people benefiting from the awards by virtue of their existing land holdings in Entwistle. The location of the lands enclosed is given on the accompanying map

Enclosure award for Cranberry Moss

Map No	Persons	Status	Address	Property in Entwistle that qualifies for the award	a	r	p
1	Robert Heywood	Gent	The Pike, Bolton	Edge or Kirkman, Tom Barn, Higher Barn, Leech	129	2	34
2	Ralph Knowles	Esquire	Bolton	Holdens, Long Barn, Simons Flat Meadow, Sheep Cote & wood plantation	187	2	15
3	Eccles Sharrock	Manuf	Darwen	Half of Edge Foot and Edge Fold	22	0	34
4	John Heywood	Gent	Failsworth.	Hall tenement or New House	58	1	10
5	Walker Hulton	Gent	Ainsworth.	Rosbottoms or Ramwells	25	0	0
6	Thomas Whitehead	Gent	Manchester	The Cote	24	1	32
7	John Barlow	Farmer	Entwistle	Lower Crow Trees & Entwistle Hall	33	3	33
8	William Entwistle	Gent	Darwen	Bolton & Bolton Barn	46	1	2
9	John Cross	Cotton Spinner	Bolton	Whittlestone Head (part)	34	2	7
10	James Barlow Sen.	Farmer	Entwistle	Whittackers	20	0	0
11	John Barlow[1]	Farmer	Entwistle	Lower Crow Trees	23	1	0
12	James Barlow Jun	Farmer	Entwistle	Higher Crow Trees	18	3	0
13	George Dixon & wife	Farmer	Entwistle	Whittlestone Head (farmland)	23	1	3
14	John Hamer	Gent	Preston	Whittlestone Head	27	0	17
15	Joseph Yates	Farmer	Entwistle	Whittlestone Head (part)	9	0	19½
16	James Yates	Farmer	Entwistle	Whittlestone Head and Jacketmans	12	3	25½

Enclosure award for Aushaw Moss

Map No	Person	Status	Address	Property in Entwistle that qualified for the award	a	r	p
17	John Yates	Farmer	Entwistle	Whittlestone Head (part)	28	0	25
18	George Yates	Farmer	Entwistle	Whittlestone Head (part)	27	2	0
19	[1]Aspdens etc		Entwistle	Pike House	50	3	5
	[2]Robert Knowles		Liverpool				
20	[2]James Kay		Warburton Pendlebury	Round Barn	56	2	14
	[2]Robert Knowles	Yeoman	Liverpool				
21	John Knowles	Yeoman	Turton	Wayoh	92	3	11
	Jane Knowles	Spinster	Turton				
22	George Slater	Gent	Holmes, Sharples	Wayoh	55	0	0
23							
24	William Rostron	Gent	Edgworth	Clough Bottom & Wayoh (part)	32	0	15
25	James Winder	Solicitor	Tonge	Know Mill	13	1	30
	William Rostron	Gent	Edgworth				
26	John D Thompson	Clerk	Barnett, Herts.	Lower Aushaw	16	2	16
27	James Kay	Gent	Turton Tower	Entwistle Hall Croft[3]	129	0	9

[1] Includes John Aspden, Nicholas Aspden, William Aspden, Thomas Aspden, Robert Aspden, Robert Greenwood, his wife Charlotte Greenwood, Robert Aspden, John Wilson, his wife Alice Wilson, Henry Aspden, and Aspden Aspden, all farmers of Entwistle; Betty Aspden and Ann Aspden, spinsters of Entwistle.

[2] Trustees of John Knowles Senior of Turton

[3] Also includes Higher House Fold and parts of Edge Foot, Edge Fold, and Top o' th' Edge.

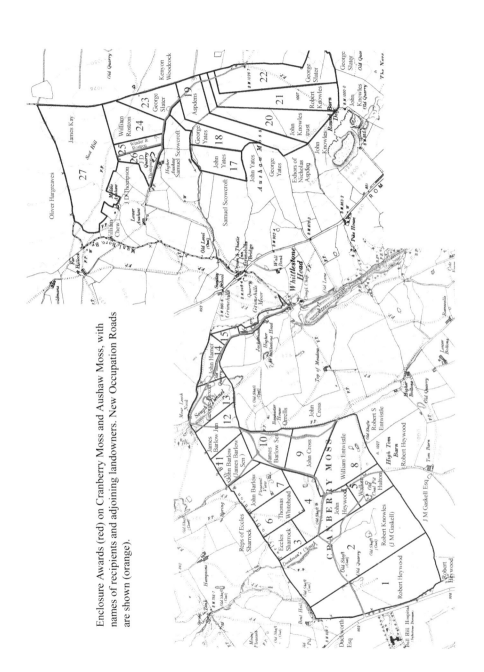

Enclosure Awards (red) on Cranberry Moss and Aushaw Moss, with names of recipients and adjoining landowners. New Occupation Roads are shown (orange).

119

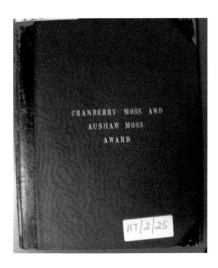

Enclosure award document for Cranberry Moss and Aushaw Moss, 1860.

Joseph Yates of Entwisle, Farmer	15	1	2	.	Whole of east fence and fence adjoining Number 16 allotment	.	5	3	Part of Whittlestone Head	9	.	19½	
James Yates of Entwisle, Farmer	16	2	.	19	Whole of east fence from C to A on Map from D to Number 15 Allotment	.	7	6	Whittlestone Head and Jacketmans	12	3	20½	
					Aushaw Moss									
John Yates of Entwisle, Farmer	17	7	.	30	Whole of fence adjoining Number 18 allotment				Part of Whittlestone Head	28	.	20½	

Details of the enclosure award showing the lands awarded and the qualifying holdings.

CHAPTER XII NOTEWORTHY INHABITANTS SINCE 1800

12.1 GENERAL

In the early 1800s many affluent businessmen invested in properties in the township of Entwistle but few chose to live there. Some exceptions, who no doubt valued the rural setting and railway facilities, included the Heywood family of Bolton, the Barlows of Edgworth and the Haslam family from Bolton.

Also in the 1795-7 enclosure of Edgworth Moor, a Mr Edmund Howarth of Turton, attorney, purchased rights and shares in respect of various properties in Entwistle, nineteen in all, which included Pike House and Clough Bottom Farms bought from William Entwistle and several turbarys (the right to dig peat) from Joseph Entwistle. In the early 1800s large parts of Entwistle Manor came into the ownership of other wealthy families, Thomas Whitehead, merchant; Robert Haywood, millowner and financier; Thomas Kay, attorney; Roger Hamer, yeoman; and George Withers Esq, surviving trustee of John Lawson deceased. Between them these gentlemen owned two thirds of the manor, some 42 properties. Although many of their tenants were still called Entwistle, the status of this great family name had clearly diminished.

At the dawn of the twentieth century uncertain times arrived in Entwistle, with periods of full employment followed by desperate poverty. The most prosperous times were during the two World Wars, with Know Mill and its workforce of more than five hundred on full production. The brickworks and stone quarry were also in full production up until the General Strike in 1926, but the local industries declined thereafter and Entwistle tended to revert to a mainly rural and agricultural community. Farms in the district were owned by families that included the Dixons, Horsefields, Mittons, Mares, Sharples and Pickups. Entwistle was still an isolated area and even in the 1930s people still travelled great distances on foot, to church, to work and to school.

By 1940 there were some twenty three farms working in Entwistle. They were only smallholdings, and many of the farmers supplemented their income with other jobs. During both wars some land was taken over by the Ministry of Defence for use as a shooting range and training area, as was Round Barn Quarry in WWII.

12.2   JOHN BARLOW AND ENTWISTLE CHAPEL

John Barlow, 1817-1870, of Crow Trees House, in his will of 7th April 1867, left a plot of land at the western corner of the Chequers Field, adjacent to Entwistle Old Hall, for the erection of a non-conformist chapel for the religious instruction and benefit of people of Entwistle.

The chapel, built in 1872, was just 6 feet away from John Barlow's grave. He was the first person to be buried in that spot followed by his sister-in-law, Mrs Sarah Barlow of Lower Crow Trees, aged 59, and his brother James Barlow in February 1880 aged 61.

This building was the centre of village life and provided socials, concerts, early picture shows and a venue for religious activities. When it was first built, it was named the Union Sunday School and attended by people of different denominations, but it later became more closely identified with Wesleyan Methodism.

The first recorded baptism, on May 21st 1893, was of James Abraham, born 11th April 1893, the son of Thomas and Alice Heys of Wayoh Fold Farm, Entwistle. The minister was the Rev'd W Barlow Brown.

The Chapel was included in the Bolton (Wesley) Circuit and was busiest during the period of prosperity brought about by local industry, particularly the Know Mill Print Works.

In the chapel book of 1884 entitled *'Wesleyan Methodist Register, Entwistle'*, charges for grave plots in front of the chapel were 15 shillings, up the sides were 10 shillings and opening up of graves cost 8s 6d. The minister's fee was 2s 6d., and that of the caretaker was 2s. Charges in a list of 1900, signed by Rev. Antony Barrass Shaw, were: opening a grave £1, minister's fee 5s, caretaker's fee 5s. One entry sadly records the death in May 1905 of Miss Elizabeth Harman Shaw of Holly Bank Cottages, Rev Shaw's daughter, aged 6½ years. Afterwards Rev Shaw and his wife went to live at the 'Top of the Steps Cottage'. The burial register records many sad cases of infant mortality, with more listed during the 1920s when hunger and long periods of unemployment occurred in Entwistle, particularly at Round Barn. The Reverend Shaw was a very benign minister. Many children died aged only 2, 3 or 4 years and his charges for these occasions, normally 4 shillings for a full service, were only 2 shillings and no charge at all for a stillbirth. He died in 1934 at the age of 63 and was buried in his daughter's grave as was his wife Margaret Agnes who died aged 70 in June 1938.

The Non-Conformist Chapel at Entwistle, built in 1872.

'Top of the Steps Cottage', home of Rev Antony Barrass Shaw.

Over a period of 80 years 73 burial plots were sold. The last persons to be buried at the chapel were Mrs Edith Alice Johnson aged 77 of 8 Walton Fold in 1951, Mr Edward Johnson aged 77 of Walton Fold in 1952 and lastly Mr Thomas Berry aged 79, of 6 Holly Bank, on July 25th 1957. Mr Berry had spent most of his working life at Know Mill Printing Co.

The Johnson family had moved to Round Barn in the 1920s. During the depression of 1925-26, when the quarry, including various cottages, buildings and farms, were sold, the Johnsons bought two of the Walton Fold cottages, the Duke of Wellington Inn and the old workhouse. Mr and Mrs Johnson retired in 1940 after a lifetime of farming and moved to Walton Fold.

The last baptism was of Keith, son of Kenneth and Joyce Nelson, 1 Holly Bank, Entwistle, on November 30th 1958. The Minister was the Rev'd Tom T Williams.

The Chapel closed in August 1963. *'Consent to Sell'* was authorised by the Methodist Conference and the Trustees conveyed the property to Mr C A Wilde of Entwistle Hall. The sale was agreed at a price of £400 less charges to the solicitors and surveyors A settlement price of £346-2s-0d was finally accepted by the Trustees on condition that the premises were to be used for dwelling house purposes. The last Trustees meeting was held August 4th, 1966 prior to the sale. A memorial plaque from the Chapel listing the men who served in the First World War was moved to the Edgworth Methodist Church in 1963.

WW1 memorial tablet from Entwistle Chapel now displayed at Edgworth Methodist Church.

124

12.3   HOLLY BANK

Entwistle has seen little in the way of speculative house building, even on a small scale. Arguably the first person to build domestic houses for rent was Mr John Burford Barlow, colliery proprietor, of Higher Crow Trees Estate. He was the son of James Barlow the younger who died on the 7th September 1880 owning one third of Entwistle Hall and Higher Crow Trees.

The development was possibly at the behest of Know Mill Printing Co, situated less than a hundred yards away. Building started about December 1880 and the first tenant of the development is listed as Mr William Rostron, the owner of Know Mill in 1882. The land covered in total approximately 9 acres in what was formerly called the Chequers Field, close by Entwistle Old Hall. The total annual rent was £165 and the lease was signed by both *'the said J.B.Barlow of the one part and the said Know Mill Printing Co of the other part'*.

In 1882 Mr John Burford Barlow and Mr William Rostron signed a lease of 10th November 1882 for the term of 19 years, for six small terraced cottages and four large houses. One house (Holly Bank) was occupied by *'Mr William Simpson, Head of the Printing Co., herein mented'* (the works manager). Holly Bank House was traditionally the home of Know Mill's manager until the late 1920s when a more modern house was built in the mill grounds, complete with gardens and greenhouse.

1884 saw a change of fortune for Mr Barlow. On 17th April 1884 he secured a mortgage of £2,500, with interest payable at 4¼% on his Higher Crow Trees Estate, the lender being a Miss Eleanor Jane Skelton, spinster of Southport. The abstract of the title reads: *'Firstly all that measse and tenements situated in Entwistle in the sd county of Lancaster now commonly called by the name of High Crow Trees, and also including and consisting of a farmhouse and cottages, farm buildings, land comprising 18 acres or thereabouts, Crow Tree House. Also estimated 9 acres of the measure after the rate of 64 sq. yds to the perch or thereabouts* [Cheshire Acres] *of land on which stands six cottages compt with gardings lying in front and the yard lying at the back, plus four large houses, let on lease to the Know Mill Printing Co in 1882 for the term of 19 yrs. At a rent of £165 p.a.'*

On the 8th August 1887 a second mortgage was agreed against the Crow Trees Estate. This indenture was made between the said Mr J B Barlow now of Parsonage Lane, Deansgate, Manchester (coal merchant) of the one part and Charles Frederick Yorke of West View, Croxley Green, Rickmansworth, Hertfordshire (gentleman) on the other part, for consideration of a loan of £700 with interest at 5%. Mr Barlow never managed to redeem his property.

The Barlow family had owned property in Bolton, Edgworth, Entwistle and Turton for over a hundred years, but John Burford Barlow was not a successful businessman and only managed to pay the interest on loans of £3,200 over a period of ten years secured on the estate. On 1st July 1892, now as a colliery manager and living in Highfield Road, Chesterfield, he agreed for the sum of £225 cash plus repayment of the outstanding loan of £700 and the mortgage of £2,500 owing to Miss E J Skelton of Southport, that the estate pass into the ownership of Mr C F Yorke, pending the settlement of Miss Skelton's debt.

On the 23rd November 1892 *'Mr C F Yorke of Cleve Hall, Denmark Hill, London (Gentleman) did pay into the Estate of Eleanor Jane Skelton, spinster of Southport, the sum of £2500'* still outstanding on the first mortgage dated 1884, and take full and free possession of the Crow Trees estate including Holly Bank Terrace.

Mr Yorke proceeded to sell off various parcels of land and properties until 1913 when we find that on 13th December he sold all six Holly Bank cottages for a total of six hundred and sixty pounds to a Mrs Alice Ann Phillipson, wife of Mr John Phillipson, of Holly Bank, Entwistle near Bolton, stone merchant and owner of Round Barn quarry.

In 1921 Mrs A A Phillipson sold 5 of her Holly Bank cottages to her sitting tenants. The names are recorded as: No.1 William and Alice Waring: No.2 James and Dorothy Greenhalgh: No.3 James and Margaret Entwistle: No.4 Joseph and Nancy Marsden: No.5 James and Sarah Corden. In 1934 Mrs Phillipson sold No.6 to Mr Thomas Berry. Subsequently Mr and Mrs Phillipson moved to invest in a new quarrying business by the name of 'Phillipson's Mont Cliff Stone Quarries' at Georges Lane, Horwich.

12.4   JOHN HASLAM OF HASLAM MILL

Lower House was a neat, medium sized, Fifteenth Century manor house built of stone, with small mullioned windows, high gabled roof and dormer windows complete with stone flagged terrace and formal gardens, which faced due south down the Yarnsdale Valley.

In the mid 1870s a Bolton man, Mr William Haslam, grandson of John Haslam (1771-1820), the founder of Haslam's textile business in Halliwell, lived with his family at White Bank House, Deane. William used Lower House as a summer residence for his family in Entwistle. From Easter until September he, his wife Mary and children would decamp to this lovely spot overlooking Entwistle Reservoir.

In the summer, William Haslam travelled each day to Bolton by train from Entwistle station. As a Senior Director of John Haslam and Co Ltd, he took his duties very seriously. He had four cotton mills to manage and a workforce in excess of 2,000 people. On Thursdays and Fridays he and his brother John would be found at the Manchester Cotton Exchange buying and selling cloth and raw cotton.

The 1920s saw great changes in the Lancashire cotton trade and as a consequence John Haslam and Co Ltd was sold to the Amalgamated Cotton Mills Trust (1920). Lower House was sold to the Bolton Corporation Water Department and demolished in 1923.

Lower House (Haslams), once the home of William Haslam with Mrs Haslam in the garden.

12.5   ROBERT HEYWOOD OF BOLTON

Robert Heywood was born in Little Bolton in 1786, the only son of John Heywood of John Heywood and Sons, quilting manufacturers (1803) of Mount Pleasant, Bury Street, Little Bolton. Their business was run from a warehouse where the weavers collected yarn which they wove in their own homes. They brought the finished pieces of cloth back every week (usually on a Monday), which the 'taker-in' (Robert Heywood) inspected and paid for. Robert Heywood would then take the cotton goods to sell at the Manchester Cotton Exchange, usually on a Saturday.

The firm prospered. John Heywood was very cautious and lived a simple life. He is said to have become rich by extreme thrift rather than the expansion of his business. Most of the family wealth was invested in loans, mainly through mortgages at high interest rates. John Heywood lent £5,100 to the Ashworth Brothers who were Quakers and cotton spinners, to help them re-equip their New Eagley Mills in 1824. When John Heywood died in May 1832 he left £36,000.

John's son, Robert Heywood, foreclosed on Jones Slaters of Crescent Bleachworks in Salford and went into bleaching for himself in 1832. Bankruptcies and foreclosures were frequent and troublesome in those times, before the introduction of the limited liability principle. One such foreclosure provided Heywood with a small estate in Entwistle, which included Oulden Fold, New Meadows House and Higher Barn Farm.

At this time, Robert Heywood along with a group of businessmen, planned to build the new Entwistle Reservoir in the Yarnsdale Valley and agreed to lend the project £10,000 at 5% interest. As mentioned previously, the venture failed when factory owners refused to pay their share of the cost. Eventually the reservoir was built on part of Heywood's considerable estate, but it was not until 1866 that he agreed to sell the Entwistle Reservoir to Bolton Corporation, for drinking water. In the sale agreement, Robert Heywood managed to insert a clause giving him sole fishing rights on the reservoir until he died. Heywood married late in 1848 at the age of 62 years to Elizabeth Shawcross who was 32 years old. They had three children, John, Mary and Robert. Robert Heywood (senior) is named as one of the principal landowners in the area in Slater's Directory of Lancashire and described as a farmer occupying New Meadows and Higher Hurst Farm (High Barn).

Robert Heywood (junior) bought the Crescent Bleachworks in Salford from his brother John and sister Mary and ran it himself for many years, travelling to Salford each day from Entwistle Station. In the evening he would return by train and then walk up Edge Lane to New Meadows House. When Robert died he had accumulated a fortune in excess of £100,000.

The Enclosure Award, mentioned earlier, of Cranberry Moss in 1859, gave Robert Heywood 129 acres of land on account of him owning estates in Entwistle. The Heywood family continued to own estates in Entwistle for nearly one hundred years.

12.6   THE WHITEHEADS

Although the Whiteheads had long been represented in Entwistle, records of a very accomplished part of the family begin with Thomas Whitehead who, as the eldest of eleven children, was born in September 1774 at Bury Street in Little Bolton. His father, Robert Whitehead, was a dyer and calenderer and founder of a bleachworks. When Robert died in February 1841, aged 88 years, his will, proved at Chester, included the strange provision that: *'My son Thomas Whitehead and his children shall not be entitled to any estate, share or interest of this my property under this my will.'*

In his twenties the young Thomas Whitehead set up as a *'Cloth Print Merchant'* in Manchester and later was involved in exporting Lancashire textiles and machinery to the Americas. He lived in a fine house at Culcheth near Leigh and owned a large villa in Kent. By 1800 he had started to buy property in Entwistle. In 1810 he bought Sheep Cote Farm, (now Whitehead Cote Farm), a one up and one down shepherd's cottage and changed it into a farmhouse extended to include a barn and shippon for eight cows. It was let for £12 per year mainly to members of his family. Being part of a very large family and relatively affluent, Thomas was in a position to help many members of his family financially.

1850 saw the death of his nephew Richard Whitehead of Whitehead Cote Farm, leaving his widow Ann (nee Yates) in desperate straits. She was described as a widow aged 38, a check cloth weaver and farmer with a son of 13 called David, described as a farmer, and 6 daughters, (Deborah 12, a weaver; Jane 10, a spinner; Margaret 8, a hand loom weaver; Alice 5, Sarah 3 and Betty 2). On hearing of their desperate plight Thomas Whitehead gave Ann money that enabled her to buy 5 cottages in Darwen. She let four of these and retained the other for herself which enabled the family to live a more prosperous life.

Thomas Whitehead's will was long and rather complex. Suffice to say that there were many bequests. He had 96 nephews, nieces and cousins and left them £450 each. He also left many thousands of pounds to good causes including The Children's Homes, Manchester Infirmary and the Royal Lifeboat Fund.

His descendants included Robert Whitehead, born 3 January 1823 at Mount Pleasant, between Bolton and Darcy Lever. He was a famous engineer and inventor, described as a saviour or a sinner, depending on whether or not you were a hapless soul on the receiving end of the torpedo, which he invented. Much of his working life had been spent away from his homeland in the industrial centres of Europe, his life being a mixture of good fortune, brilliance and sheer hard work.

Robert did well at primary school and passed entrance requirements for the grammar school, now Bolton School, but left at 14 to start an apprenticeship at Ormond and Sons, Engineers, in Manchester where his uncle was manager. Whitehead had already shown a flare for engineering and technical drawing, whilst still at school and evening classes at the Mechanics Institute in Manchester were spent learning draughtsmanship. He joined Philips Taylor and Sons in Marseilles at the age of 21 and later worked in Milan then in Trieste at the Strudnoff engineering works. Having been invited to Fiume, a major naval base and shipbuilding centre for the Austro-Hungarian Empire, to design naval craft, he was then asked to work on the development of a type of floating torpedo which was little more than a self-propelled explosive boat. Robert Whitehead could see the potential but decided to start again from scratch to build the aforementioned torpedo. With the help of his son John, he succeeded in 1866 and his invention became an effective marine weapon with sufficient explosive power and accuracy to sink steel-hulled ships. This self propelled underwater bomb (known as the 'Devil's Device') sank countless naval and merchant ships during both World Wars and killed thousands of sailors. Robert Whitehead died in 1905 at the age of 82, an exceedingly wealthy man.

His grandson John Whitehead went to live at Whitehead Cote Farm, Entwistle and had 5 daughters and 1 son. Agatha Whitehead, Robert's great granddaughter, married Georg Von Trapp in Austria in 1911. Agatha died at the age of 32 of diphtheria in 1922 leaving her husband to bring up their seven children alone. He employed a governess, Maria, who taught the children to sing and they later became world famous in the musical 'The Sound of Music.'

Robert Heywood of New Meadows, businessman financier and one time mayor of Bolton.

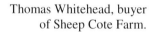

Thomas Whitehead, buyer of Sheep Cote Farm.

Robert Whitehead, inventor of the torpedo.

Whitehead Cote (formerly Sheep Cote) Farm, one time residence of John Whitehead.

Armsgrove Farm: one time home of the Mr Arthur Taylor Mitton.

12.7　THE MITTONS AND OTHERS

From 1923 until 2004 the most prominent family living in Entwistle were the Mittons. Arthur Taylor Mitton married Emmie Jane Evans at St. Anne's Church, Turton on June 3 1914 and lived on the smallholding of Armsgrove, which stands alongside the ancient, now defunct highway of Edge Lane, now just over the township boundary in Turton, but once part of Entwistle Manor.

Armsgrove Farm, formerly called Hermit Grove Farm, (sometimes Armsgreace, Armegreave or Army Grove) had been part of the Tyldesley family estate in 1657 and was sold by them, together with 16 other farms to John Entwistle and John Norbury. In 1695 this small estate, then commonly called 'Ould House' of the Overhouse Tenements, was sold by the last of the Norbury family, Mrs Rebecca Thomasson, *nee* Norbury, to John Brandwood, of Entwistle, for £140 of which £120 was paid in cash. John and his son James Brandwood were builders and by the time James Brandwood died on 19th July 1716 the 'Ould House' section of the Overhouses Estate had been increased in size to four tenements which included the Hermit Grove Farm.

By 1730 the farm had come under the jurisdiction of Sir Humphrey Chetham who was then Lord of the Manor of Turton. It was owned by a Mr Edward Brown, an absentee landlord, and was rented to a Mr James Wood, farmer, for 6s-8d per year. The farm then consisted of a small cottage, barn and 50a 0r 11p of land (Cheshire measure). James Wood lived there for 11 years. For tax purposes, the farm was valued in 1750 at £116-13s-4d plus a standing grove of timber at £24-6s-6d.

The farmhouse, built by John Brandwood in sandstone with a split stone roof, was renamed in 1770 Army Greaves Farm, because three pieces of armour were found in a nearby field, possibly from the Civil War. In 1811 the barn adjacent to the farmhouse fell down and at great expense the Brandwoods rebuilt it for £95 3s 3d (see James Brandwood's account of rebuilding expenses).

Mr and Mrs Mitton moved to Entwistle Hall Farm in 1923 to raise dairy cattle, pigs and poultry on 40 acres. In the 1920s Lancashire was badly hit by unemployment and by the general strike and coalminers strike. Money was tight but with thrift and careful housekeeping the Mittons survived. Mr Mitton started a milk round and also sold eggs from door to door while Mrs Mitton organized farmyard duties between their six children. Tasks were performed before and after school and as a consequence they had enough food to lead a healthy lifestyle but very little money to spend. They milked 15 cows in the morning before school and again after school. Milk was sold to the Bolton Co-op Dairies in Kay Street; kits would be collected at the top of the lane and taken to Entwistle Railway Station en route for Bolton. Also with almost 1000 free range hens about the farm there was no shortage of jobs for the children.

Arthur Mitton's interests were varied and wide ranging. In his spare time he bred poultry to show standards; he had a preference for Rhode Island Reds, Blue Leghorns and Marans. He travelled far and wide to poultry shows, including those in Darwen, Manchester, Lancaster and London, and had literally dozens of certificates and prizes, not to mention silver cups. Later in life Mr Mitton became a well respected judge at the Great Manchester Poultry Shows and he also took a keen interest in local history. Mrs Mitton's interests included reading, listening to the wireless and knitting (mainly socks, not surprisingly with 6 children to provide for). She had a life-long interest in dog breeding and specialized in Shetland Sheepdogs and miniature Collies.

Their youngest child Alfred Mitton was the only one born (1927) at Entwistle Hall Farm. He attended Hob Lane School, leaving at the age of 14 to work at Know Mill. After the war at the age of 17, Alf started full-time work on his father's farm. Most of the heavy work was done with the help of horses; Alf remembers two Clydesdale Cross Shires used for ploughing, horse drawn grass mowing, haymaking and milk delivery by 'Pilkington' milk float. Alf took over the farm when Mr and Mrs Mitton retired in 1967 and went to live in Hollybank Cottages, not more than 50 yards from Entwistle Hall Farm and just near enough to give a helping hand in times of emergencies.

In the 1970s small milking herds became unprofitable. The Ministry of Agriculture persuaded most dairy farms to change to beef production and so with the dexterity of a man raised on the land, and encouraged and assisted by his wife Barbara, Alf went into beef farming together with pigs and poultry. Barbara continued breeding Shetland Sheepdogs and they carried on farming at the Hall, helped in later years by their daughter Diane (Mitton) Baron until Alf and Barbara retired in 2002 to spend their retirement in the centre of village life at Barlow Court in Edgworth.

After 800 years of continual farming, Entwistle Hall is now divided into 4 private residences and takes on a more tranquil role. The barn across the yard has been converted into a house. Across the the railway line another detached barn, once belonging to the farm, has been converted into a beautiful house called Mitton Hall, a fitting tribute to the Brandwoods.

Mitton Hall in 2008, a 17th century barn conversion at Entwistle Hall Farm.

Alfred Mitton, son of Arthur at Entwistle Hall Farm

Marriage of Arthur T Mitton to Emmie J Evans in 1914. Afterwards they lived at Armsgrove Farm.

Arthur and Emmie Mitton on their retirement in 1967.

100th birthday of Emmie Jane Mitton.

Some other Entwistle people known to the author are recorded in the following photographs, together with soldiers at the rifle range and pupils at Hob Lane School.

Mrs Hatzer with her eldest son at Crow Tree Cottages.

Men of the 5th Battalion, the Loyal Regiment in 1939 at Entwistle Rifle Range alongside Broadhead Brook, near Wayoh Bridge.

137

'Lugano', one of a group of five bungalows on Overshores Road and home since 1929 to Henry Slater and his family. The house was named by an aunt who was reminded of a visit to Switzerland by the surrounding scenery.

The Slater children at Hob Lane School in 1931.The children remember meeting Henry when he came out of Know Mill where he was a calico printer.

Henry and Margaret Slater with children Cyril, Olive and twins Hilda and Harold, 1920.

The Postman: Jim Horsfield

Postman Jim Horsfield about to retire after 34 years of local service. Jim remembers each day before school taking two baskets of eggs to Entwistle Station destined for shops in Darwen.

Jim Horsfield with John Dixon of Round Barn Farm, 1990s.

Hob Lane School

Photograph of children at Hobb Lane School, Edgworth, which many from Entwistle attended.

Other Entwistle children at Hob Lane School.

APPENDIX 1 PROTESTATION LIST FOR ENTWISTLE

A countrywide protest against 'arbitrary and tyrannical government' was organized in 1641/2, which all Englishmen over 18 had to sign. The list for Entwistle is as follows:

George Aspden
John Aspinwall
James Banester
John Banester
Edward Bolton
Richard Bolton
Oliver Brendwood
Roger Brendwood
Thomas Catterall
Alexander Entwisley
Elllis Entwisley
Hugh Entwisley
John Entwisley Jnr
John Entwisley the older
John Entwisley the oldest
Ralphe Entwisley
Thomas Entwisley Jnr
Thomas Entwisley
Edward Fogge
William Greenhalgh
Arthur Greenalgh
Thurstan Greenalgh
Richard Greenhalghe

John Greenhalgh
James Haydocke
Edmund Horrocke
James Horrocke
Alexander Kaie
Arthur Kaie
Arthur Kaye Jnr.
James Kaye
John Kaye the older
John Kay Jnr
Martin Kaie the older
Martin Kaye younger
James Knowles
James Longworthe
James Longworthe the older
John Longworthe
Ralphe Longworth Jnr.
Richard Longworthe
Francis Norburie
Thomas Orrel
Christopher Rawstorne J
John Shipplebothome

WITNESSES:
James Warberton, John Welch, John Whiticar
Jacobus Bradshawe, Minister of Turton?
Thomas Grynaulghe, Constabl
Alexander Haworth, Christopher Rawstone , Constables of Edgeworth.

APPENDIX 2   HEARTH TAX RETURNS FOR ENTWISTLE

The Hearth Tax, introduced in 1662, was collected every six months until 1689. The tax for residents was 2 shillings per annum for each hearth in their property, except paupers, people in houses worth less than 20 shillings annually, or those not paying poor rates. The township constable was responsible for drawing up lists of inhabitants classified into tax payers and those exempt.

The 1665 return lists householders classified into chargeable and non chargeable categories. Unfortunately the return in that year did not distinguish Entwistle as a separate township. Returns for 1666 and 1673 are readily available but list only chargeable hearths. The 1673 return is not clearly written and some names are abbreviated, where this occurs the correct name is included.

1666		1673	
Householder	Hearths	Householder	Hearths
Francis Norbury	7	Noris [Norris] Norbury	4
John Entwistle	3	Fra [Francis] Norbury	1
Hugh Entwistle	3	Robt Norbury	1
William Horrocks	3	James Knowles	1
Roger Brandwood	4	Dd [David] Whitehead	1
Peter Kay	1	Roger Brandwood	4
Peter Bradley	1	Christ Horoc [Christopher Horrocks]	2
Thomas Aspinall	1	Thurst Cester [Thurstan Chester ?]	1
Henry Horrocks	1	Thos Entwisle	1
John Kay	2	Wm Orhill [Orrell]	1
James Knowles	1	Matyn Key [Martin Kay]	1
Alexander Kay	1	Thos Entwisle	1
John Kay	1	George Longeworth	1
Thomas Entwistle	1	John Bradw [Brandwood]	1
John Longworth	1	? Greenehouge [Greenhalgh]	1
George Longworth	1	Hen Horroc [Horrocks]	1
John Brandwood	1	Ellis Rochell [Rossal]	1
Christopher Rawstorne [Rostron]	1	James Key	1
Amos Greenhalgh	1	John Key	1
John Entwistle	1	Thos Aspinall	1
		John Entwisle	1
		Peter Key	1
		John Entwisle smith	1
		Peter Bradley	1
		Hugh Entwisle	1
		Ed Fyge [Fogg ?]	1

APPENDIX 3   POLL TAX RETURN FOR ENTWISTLE

There were several Poll Taxes in the late seventeenth century all of which involved persons over the age of 16 (other than the poor) in paying tax depending broadly on their status. The tax was assessed by township in Lancashire and the return for Entwistle for 1678 is given below with the original spelling:

A true list of all the names and surnames of such persones in the Hamell of Entwisle who are chargable by the acts of parlement to pay polle money
May 6 1678

	£ - s - d
Roger Brandwood and his wife and three Children	*00-05-00*
Willaim Horroks and his wife and one Child	*00-03-00*
widdow Entwistle and one Child	*00-02-00*
Ann Entwisle and one Child	*00-02-00*
John Entwisle	*00-01-00*
John Entwisle and his wif and one Child	*00-03-00*
David whithead and his wif and one Child	*00-03-00*
John Brendwood and his wif and one Child	*00-03-00*
Henry Longworth and his wif and one Child	*00-03-00*
Elies grinough [Ellis Greenhalgh ?]	*00-01-00*
Alexad [Alexander] *Entwisle*	*00-01-00*
Lawanc [Lawrence] *Witticare and his wife*	*00-02-00*
James Knowles and his wif and one Childe	*00-03-00*
widow Key [Kay] *and her daughter*	*00-02-00*
James Key	*00-01-00*
Peter Key and his wif and one sonne	*00-03-00*
Thomas Aspinall and his sonne	*00-02-00*
Peter Bradly and his wif	*00-02-00*
widow Norbury and two Children	*00-03-00*
Thomas Hooge [Hogg] *servant*	*00-02-00*
John Wadington	*00-01-00*
Thomas Tarkinton	*00-01-00*
Clem Lowe	*00-01-00*
Sarah Horrockes	*00-01-00*
Ralph Entwisle the assessor	*00-01-00*
	2-12-00

wiliam ? Colektor for Entwisle

Assesed by me Ralph Entwisle

The above table includes the last mention of the Norbury family in Entwistle after 150 years. It also provides the first documentary reference to the Tarkington family and, presumably, the farm of that name.

BIBLIOGRAPHY AND REFERENCES

The Victoria County History of Lancashire, Vol 5: 1911.
Baines History of Lancashire, Vol 1: 1868.
History Directory and Gazetteer of Lancashire, Edward Baines: 1824.
The Templars, Piers Paul Read:1999.
History of the Entwistle Family, Bannister Grimshaw: 1924.
The Journal of Nicholas Assheton, F R Rains, Ed: 2009.
The Civil War in Lancashire, Stephen Bull: 2009.
Correspondence of Edward Third Earl of Derby, Chetham Society NS19: 1890.
Bolton-le-Moors and townships in the Parish, P A Whittle: 1855
History of Bolton, J Scholes: 1892.
Progress on Roads, Charles Walker: 1966.
Robert Heywood of Bolton, 1786-1868, WE Brown: 1970.
The Bolton, Blackburn, Clitheroe and West Yorkshire Railway, WD Tattersall: 1973.
Dictionary of British History by S.H. Steinberg: 1963.
Halls Circuits and Ministers: 1912
Lancs Local History, (OU Historical Soc) No 14: 1999

Use has also been made of the following sources:-

Publications Nos 7 and 20 of Turton Local History Society.
TLHS archives: mainly for the Brandwood family papers and The Edgworth Gazette:
1980.
Lancashire Record Office, Tyldeseley Papers by B Grimshaw.
Lancashire Record Office, Turton Records particularly ref UDTu19 including:-
Admission register Goose Cote Workhouse, 1847 and Chetham Trust Daybook.
Registers of Births, Deaths and Marriages
Records at the Barlow Institute, Edgworth.
Documents held privately including the Briggs papers, various property deeds, indentures
and correspondence with the author.
Bolton Archives: documents relating to Entwistle, Round Barn, the McCreary family,
and Goose Cote Workhouse
Darwen Library, Local Studies Collection.

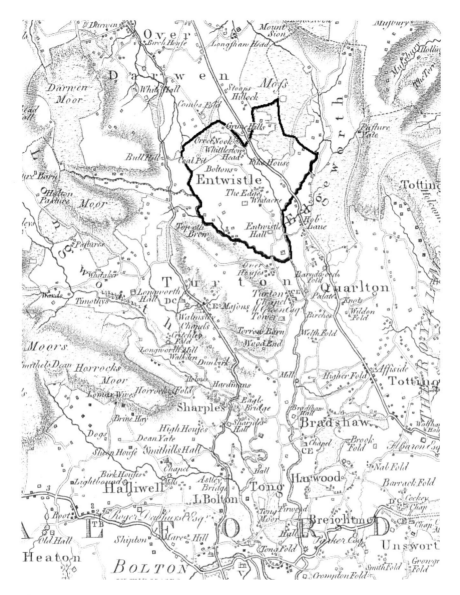

Yates map of 1785 showing the Township of Entwistle (outlined in black) and surrounding area before any turnpike roads, bleachworks, reservoirs or railways had been constucted. The Roman Road is clearly shown passing right through township and the old highway between Bolton, Darwen and Blackburn runs near the western boundary.

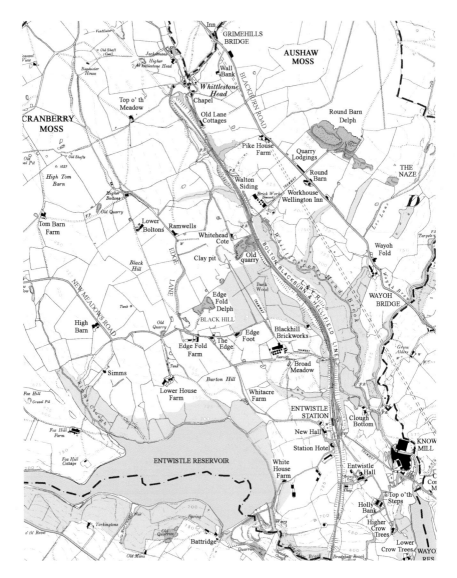

Map of Entwistle on 6 inch OS base of 1912.

146